The Pirchei Shoshanim Pictorial Series

סדר ברכת המזון
Birkas Hamazon

Commentary by Rabbi Daniel Channen
Illustrations by Rabbi Dovid Goldschmidt

Pirchei Publishing
164 Village Path / P.O. Box 708
Lakewood, New Jersey 08701
(732) 370-3344
www.shulchanaruch.com

Product Produced & Compiled by YPS:
Rabbi Shaul Danyiel & Rabbi Ari Montanari
www.lionsden.info/YPS

פרחי שושנים
PIRCHEI SHOSHANIM

Midos tovos. Yiras Shamayim. Ahavas Hatorah.

These are the values that we, as parents and educators, hope to inculcate in our children. But the demands are great, and resources are limited. There is a growing need for innovative materials that can capture our children's attention in an ever-changing world.

This is the task of Pirchei Shoshanim.

Pirchei Shoshanim began as children's groups, founded sometime in the middle 1700s in Eastern Europe. Children who were members of Pirchei Shoshanim would visit parents on the day of the newly born son's bris and enroll the infant in the organization. The parents would then donate charity for the purchase of Jewish books. In this way, the children would collect enough to buy a new Shas, Rambam, or Mishnayos.

Today, Pirchei Shoshanim provides a pool of innovative educational materials to teachers and educators around the world at no charge. Everyone in the world has access to our full series of illustrated lessons on various subjects, such as shmiras halashon; halachos of Shabbos; weekly parshah sheets, focusing on midos; and a complete picture series of Pirkei Avos.

Pirchei Shoshanim has now developed many forums to serve parents and educators as well as children. Today, Pirchei Shoshanim primarily focuses on addressing problems that arise from contemporary society.

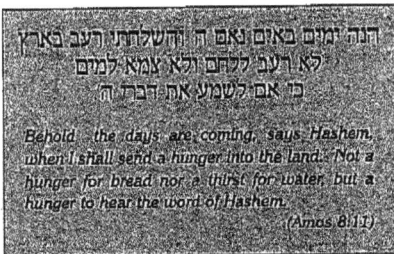

הנה ימים באים נאם ה והשלחתי רעב בארץ
לא רעב ללחם ולא צמא למים
כי אם לשמע את דברי ה

Behold, the days are coming, says Hashem, when I shall send a hunger into the land. Not a hunger for bread nor a thirst for water, but a hunger to hear the word of Hashem.

(Amos 8:11)

Pirchei Shoshanim's internal database for shidduchim allows shadchanim to exchange names and information in strict confidentiality. Nearly 1000 names have been submitted to date, making it the largest database of its type in the world.

Another pressing issue is the increasing number of children who have strayed from their heritage. Pirchei Shoshanim is in the process of developing material and programs to help parents, children and teachers deal with this problem. Expert teachers and professionals with years of experience are being recruited to address this modern-day plague. Pirchei Shoshanim is seeking solutions to encourage parents and children to renew their relationships, while growing in their commitment to their heritage.

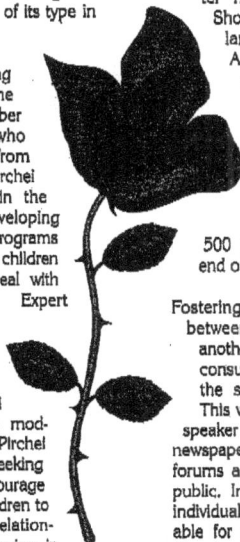

Pirchei Shoshanim women's forum, called Eishes Chayil, deals with contemporary issues for Jewish women. Feature articles are on topics such as Jewish law, the Torah portion of the week, tips for parents in dealing with family and home, recipes, and more. The Eishes Chayil newsletter, sent out weekly, also distributes names for Tehillim, while addressing many real-life issues.

The success of the Avos V'Bonim program in Israel, in which nearly 20,000 fathers and sons learn together after Shabbos in the winter months, has led Pirchei Shoshanim to develop a similar program in North America. Pirchei Shoshanim will use its existing father and son learning programs in North Miami Beach and Los Angeles as the launching point for a nationwide campaign, in which we hope to create more than 500 learning programs by the end of the coming school year.

Fostering good relationships between husband and wife is another important issue. A top consultant has recently joined the staff of Pirchei Shshanim. This world-renowned author and speaker and internationally known newspaper columnist will be offering forums and articles for the general public. In addition, he will answer individual questions and will be available for one-on-one consultations. Many have already benefited from his help, and we plan on increasing our efforts in this area.

PIRCHEI SHOSHANIM'S ACCOMPLISHMENTS:

·KOLLEL DAF YOMI- A full time Kollel for learning Daf Yomi. A complete synopsis of the Daf Yomi in English is supplied to all participants, including background, insights, review, and a point by point summary. The Kollel, which is based in Yerushalayim, started at Mesechta Chullin and is now current with the Daf. Over a thousand people receive this information daily.

·CHOFETZ CHAIM- The daily page from the popular sefer A Lesson A Day is sent out to thousands of people around the world, both in Hebrew and English. It is a complete pictorial concept of how to protect oneself from falling into the pitfalls of speaking Loshon Hara.

·PUBLICATIONS- Pirchei Shoshanim is recognized as a major publisher of Jewish educational material. Leading the list of recently published works are the classic Iggeres HaRamban, Sefer Taharas Haloshon, The Yom Kippur Avodah, The Laws of the Day, How to Make Shabbos, Eishes Chayil, and the recently published Dik Duk Buk, with its innovative approach to teaching the Hebrew language. This remarkable textbook is fast becoming a classic in homes and schools everywhere. The latest addition to our publishing list is the Laws of Shmittah. All books are available to schools at a large discount.

·KIRUV RESOURCES - Pirchei Shoshanim has consolidated twenty-five years' worth of material from Project Seed of England's archives, allowing outreach workers to quickly and easily find the information they need to help them in their invaluable work.

·JEWISH BURIAL- Pirchei Shoshanim provides the only public forum available on all aspects of Jewish burial. Thanks to our efforts, many cremations have been stopped, and a large number of buri-als were conducted properly. Pirchei Shoshanim works at informing Jewish funeral home directors of the proper laws, as well as organizing many chevrah kadishas around the world.

·CD DAF- This sophisticated CD-ROM contains the masechtos of the Daf Yomi together with thousands of links and a convenient search engine. The CD is available in English, Yiddish, Hebrew, and now French. Jews around the world now have an unmatched tool to help them keep up with Daf Yomi, no matter where they may be.

·RUSSIAN PROGRAM- For almost a decade, Pirchei Shoshanim has supported educational development in the former Soviet Union. In recent years, Pirchei Shoshanim has sent delegations to help the schools develop their learning programs in summer camps. Thousands of Mishnayos were learned during these programs, while the children felt—for the first time—that they were truly a part of Klal Yisrael. Pirchei Shoshanim is currently translating its Pictorial Series into Russian, and is working on developing further educational resources in Kiev, where two schools now provide the needs of 600 Jewish children. Plans include two additional schools and orphanages for children who need clothes, food and shelter, in addition to a Jewish education.

·EUROPEAN PROGRAM- Pirchei Shoshanim has made great inroads in bridging the language barrier. Together with it's French Partner OZAR HATORAH who provides for the needs of over 5,000 Jewish Children in Paris, Pirchei Shoshanim is having it's learning programs translated into French to help fulfill the needs of nearly 750,000 Jews who reside in France currently. With the presentation of its Shmittah Book,

Pirchei Shoshanim hopes to give encouragement to all the Jewish Schools in Great Britain, Ireland and Scotland.

LATIN AMERICA- Pirchei Shoshanim, with the introduction of its Birchat Hamazon book will be making major inroads into the Spanish speaking Jewish communities of Mexico (nearly 30,000) and Buenos Aires (almost 250,000 Jews). The communities of Panama, Caracas, Chile and Ecuador are all looking forward to this book, which will be a milestone in Jewish Education in Latin America.

·FRENCH PROGRAM- Pirchei Shoshanim works together with Ozar HaTorah to help provide the needs of over 5,000 Jewish children in Paris.

From Edmonton to New York, from Miami to Bnei Brak, Pirchei Shoshanim continues to provide children and educators with resources and material they need for a comprehensive Jewish education. Our goal is to link educators and children around the world by providing the educational tools that foster midos tovos and strengthen Jewish identity--to ensure that the chain of Jewish tradition will never be broken.

Acknowledgments

With gratitude to Hashem, Pirchei Shoshanim presents *Seder Birkas Hamazon*, the sixth volume in the *Pirchei Shoshanim Pictorial Series*. After nearly four years in the making, this work has proven to be a monumental accomplishment in helping the entire world give the appropriate thanks for their daily bread to our Creator, may His name be blessed. Eventually, we hope to publish this *Seder Birkas Hamazon* in more than 6 languages.

Pirchei Shoshanim, has teamed the talents of the world renowned artist, Rabbi Dovid Goldschmidt, with the writing of Rabbi Daniel Channen, to produce what educators, parents and children have all agreed is a most invaluable tool in helping so many understand *Birkas Hamazon*.

It is Pirchei Shoshanim's hope that this important publication will reach Jewish children all around the globe, both in the classroom and at home. Toward this end, Pirchei Shoshanim is developing an accompanying teacher's/parent's manual to further help the children's understanding of *Birkas Hamazon*.

Although our shining light HaRav HaGaon Reb Aryeh Leib Berenbaum, z"tl, was taken from us nearly five years ago, he continues to provide us with the strength, energy and determination to overcome all the obstacles we encounter. Rebbetzin Nechama Berenbaum, שתחי׳, continues to encourage us as well as playing a pivotal role in coordinating Pirchei Shoshanim's efforts in Eretz Yisrael.

The editing talents of Mrs. Elky Langer and Mrs. Rivkie Goldman are manifest in this work. Their unselfish devotion toward this project was integral in making this publication possible.

Without Mrs. Fern Scheinberg's valiant efforts and responsibility for every single aspect of this project, this work would not have come fruition. Her tireless efforts, no matter what time of the day or night, cannot be overstated. Shepsil Scheinberg has once again outdone himself with his beautiful cover design.

Our distributor, Rabbi Alexander Zissel Ellinson together with his staff at CIS Publishers, is always there to make sure all is done and done right. With the release of this *Seder Birkas Hamazon*, he has helped us reach a new milestone in Pirchei Shoshanim publications.

We hope and pray that the *Ribono Shel Olam* will continue to bless our efforts and that we may be *zocheh* to bring many more such important works into Jewish homes and schools around the world.

Pirchei Shoshanim
Yerushalayim/Lakewood
Tishrei 5761

סדר ברכת המזון

Birkas Hamazon

נְטִילַת יָדַיִם
Washing Hands Before Eating Bread

בָּרוּךְ אַתָּה ה' אֱלֹקֵינוּ מֶלֶךְ
הָעוֹלָם, אֲשֶׁר קִדְּשָׁנוּ בְּמִצְוֹתָיו,
וְצִוָּנוּ עַל נְטִילַת יָדָיִם.

Washing hands

The Rabbis considered bread so important because it is the food which satisfies a person and keeps him alive, as it says, "ולחם לבב אנוש יסעד - Bread nourishes a man's heart." (*Tehillim* 104:15) For this reason, the Rabbis decreed that a special *beracha* should be said before eating bread. The *beracha* that we say is *Hamotzi lechem min ha-aretz* - who causes bread to grow from the land. (*Shulchan Aruch Harav* 167:1)

Before eating bread we should wash our hands. In the time of the *Beis Hamikdash*, the *Kohanim* washed their hands before eating *Terumah* (grain that had been set aside for the *Kohanim*), so that the *Terumah* would not become *tamei* (spiritually impure) when they touched

it. The Rabbis made it a custom for everyone to wash their hands, for the sake of the *Kohanim*. In this way, when the *Beis Hamikdash* is rebuilt (we pray that this will happen quickly, in our days), the *Kohanim* will be in the habit of washing their hands before eating, and will not cause the *Terumah* to become *tamei*. Another reason for washing hands is cleanliness. (*Mishnah Berurah* 158:1)

Washing Hands: The cup that is used to wash the hands is first held in the left hand and water is poured on the right hand two times. Then, the cup is held in the right hand and water is poured over the left hand twice. He recites *Al Netilas Yadayim* while his hands are still wet, and then takes a towel to dry his hands. He then says *Hamotzi*, and eats a piece of bread.

1

בָּרוּךְ אַתָּה ה' אֱלֹקֵינוּ מֶלֶךְ הָעוֹלָם, הַמוֹצִיא לֶחֶם מִן הָאָרֶץ.

The amount needed in order to make the *beracha* of *Hamotzi*

Before eating bread, we wash our hands, say *Al netilas yadayim* and then *Hamotzi lechem min ha'aretz*. What do we do if we are just nibbling a little piece of bread, less than a whole slice? The Rabbis use two measurements for bread, to teach us how to know when to make certain *berachos*. The larger measurement is a *beitza*, which is about the center of a slice of rye bread.

The second measurement is a *kezayis*, approximately half of the center of a slice of rye bread. Even if we eat only a *kezayis* of bread, we should wash, say *Al netilas yadayim*, and then *Hamotzi*. This is because a *kezayis* is the part of the meal which satisfies a person's hunger. (*HaRav* Moshe Feinstein *zt"l* based on the *GR"A*) If we eat less than a *kezayis*, we should wash without saying *Al netilas yadayim*. (*Igros Moshe* 4:41) Afterwards, we say *Hamotzi* - before eating even the smallest amount of bread.

2

Salt and bread

The *Rama* says that it is a *mitzvah* to put salt on the table before reciting *Hamotzi*. This is because the table is compared to a *mizbeyach* - altar - and our meal is like a *korban* - sacrifice. Every *korban* is brought with salt. (*Orach Chayim* 167:5)

While we sit and wait for the rest of the family to wash and join us for *Hamotzi*, we are not doing mitzvos. This is the perfect time for the *Satan* to bother us and cause us harm. The *bris melach* - the agreement that was made with salt - protects us at this time. (*Mishnah Berurah* 167:32) In fact, the *Mekubalim* - Kabbalists - would dip their bread in salt three times. (*Mishnah Berurah* 167:33)

When *Birkas Hamazon* is said

The *beracha* said after a meal with bread is usually *Birkas Hamazon*.

The mitzvah from the Torah is to *bentch* when one is satisfied.(*Gemara Brachos* 20b). Even if one eats only a *kezayis*, at least half of the center of slice of rye bread, it is a rabbinical mitzvah to *bentch*. (*Gemara Brachos* 49b *Tosfoth*) According to most *poskim* this amount should be eaten within slightly more than three minutes. However the custom is that if one ate this amount of bread at any time during the meal he should *bentch*.

Tehillim

Before reciting *Birkas Hamazon*, there is a custom to say *al naharos bavel* - by the waters of Babylon (*Tehillim* 137) in order to remember the destruction of the *Beis Hamikdash*. On Shabbos and Yom Tov, and days when we do not recite *tachanun*, we do not say *al naharos bavel*. Instead we say *shir hamalos* - a song of spiritual rising (*Tehillim* 126). These are joyous days and this psalm describes the joy which we will feel when Hashem takes us out of exile.

כּוֹס שֶׁל בְּרָכָה
Bentching Over a Cup of Wine

בכבודי

Please

Bentching over a cup of wine

There is a custom to say *Birkas Hamazon* holding a cup of wine, which is called *kos shel beracha*. This is done on Shabbos and Yom Tov, at a wedding, or at a festive meal where a *minyan* (ten) of men are eating together. Even on these occasions, when one person *bentches* - says the prayer of *Birkas Hamazon* - by himself, the custom is not to *bentch* over a cup of wine. (*Mishnah Berurah* 182:16) If three people eat together, they are not required to *bentch* over a cup of wine. However, if they do so, it is considered as if they did a *mitzvah* in the best possible way. (*Mishnah Berurah* 182:4)

During the third meal of Shabbos, the custom may be different depending on the time a person begins to *bentch*. If *Birkas Hamazon* was said before the end of Shabbos, then one may drink from the *kos shel beracha* even if he does not usually *bentch* over a cup of wine. (*Mishnah Berurah* 299:14) However, if Shabbos has already ended, he should leave the *kos shel beracha* in the place where he ate the third meal, *bentch*, and return to make *havdalah* over this cup of wine. This way it is also counted as the *kos shel beracha*. (*Rivevos Efrayim* 2:117, according to *Rav* Moshe Feinstein *zt"l*)

Washing hands at the end of the meal

It is a *halacha* - Jewish law - to wash *mayim acharonim*. (After eating a meal with bread, a person must wash his hands before saying the *Birkas Hamazon*. This washing of hands is called *mayim acharonim*.) There are two reasons for this:

1. The fingers are dirty and it is not proper to make a *beracha* like this.

2. It is possible that *melach Sedom* - salt of Sodom - is still on his fingers from the meal. Even today when *melach Sedom* is rare, there is still a chance that it is mixed in with regular salt. The danger is that it can cause harm to a person's eyes if he accidentally touches them while the *melach Sedom* is on his fingers. (*Mishnah Berurah* 181:1) The Chofetz Chaim rules that even in modern times, a person should be strict about washing *mayim acharonim*. (*Mishnah Berurah* 181:22)

When a person washes for *mayim acharonim*, he should not just dampen his fingertips. The Chofetz Chaim says that a person who does only this has not done what is necessary. (*Mishnah Berurah* 181:10) Instead, a person should wash up to the second knuckle, or higher up, if it is not clean there.

דִינֵי זִימּוּן

Bentching With a Group - Laws

The laws of Bentching with a group

When three or more men, aged thirteen and older, eat together, they must *bentch* together. This group which is formed is called a *zimun*. Their praise to Hashem is considered greater, since it is done with a group. We learn this from *Mishlei* 14:28, as it is written, "In a greater number of people there is glory of the King." There are two sources for making a *zimun*. First, it is written, "When I will call out the name of Hashem, praise Hashem for his greatness." (*Devarim* 32:3) Second, it says, "Praise the name of Hashem with me, in front of many, and let us bring more honor to His Name together." (*Tehillim* 34:4) (*Mishnah Berurah* 192:1)

According to most authorities, it is a Rabbinical obligation to make a *zimun*. (*Shaar HaZion* 197:16) The laws of *zimun* are many. Here are a few basics:

1. The mitzvah of *zimun* is for a meal where bread is eaten. (*Mishnah Berurah* 193:6)

2. Three people who eat together, are required to make a *zimun*. (*Mishnah Berurah* 193:6)

3. If two people sit together and eat bread, it is a *mitzvah* to find a third person to eat with them, so they can make a *zimun*. (*Mishnah Berurah* 193:7)

4. When two people eat bread together and want to invite a third person to make a *zimun* with them, they may include him even if he does not want to eat bread, as long as he drinks (anything except water) or eats any other food with them. (*Mishnah Berurah* 197:22) This third person answers to the *zimun* and remains seated with the group until after the first *beracha*, which is *hazan es hakol*. The others, of course, continue with *Birkas Hamazon*.

5. Women cannot be counted as part of this group, even those women who are part of the family (for example, husband, wife, and son) because their requirements are different. (*Mishnah Berurah* 199:12)

6. Women must answer to a *zimun* if they ate with men. (*Mishnah Berurah* 199:17)

7

הַמְזַמֵן
Bentching with a Group - Leader

The leader of the group

Who should lead the *zimun*?

1.When a group of people sit together, each eating their own food, the honor of leading the group should be given to the *gadol bechachmah* - the wisest in learning, since no one is considered a guest. However, if there is a guest at the table, then the guest should be asked to lead the *zimun*. (*Mishnah Berurah* 201:3) We ask the guest to lead us so he can give a special blessing to his host during the last *beracha* in *Birkas Hamazon*. (*B'eir Heiteiv* 201:3)

2.When there are a few guests, the host may choose any one of them to lead the *zimun*, even if one is greater than the other. (*Mishnah Berurah* 201:4)

3. If the host is willing to give up the special *beracha* which a guest would give him, he is permitted to lead the *zimun* himself. (*Shulchan Aruch* 201:1)

4. The host may choose any person eating at his meal, even someone who is not a guest - such as a family member. (*Rama*)

5. When a *Talmid Chochom* is present he should lead *bentching* unless he gives permission for someone else to lead. When a *Kohain* is part of a *zimun*, he should lead, or we should ask his permission to lead instead of him. However, if the Torah scholar gives permission to the *Kohain* to lead, then he may lead the *zimun*. (*Shulchan Aruch* 201:2)

8

נוסַח הַזִימוּן

Bentching With a Group - Basic Text

The wording of the *Zimun*

This is the way we begin reciting the *Birkas Hamazon*:

1. LEADER BEGINS:

"רַבּוֹתַי נְבָרֵךְ"

Gentlemen, let us bentch.

2. ALL RESPOND:

"יְהִי שֵׁם ה' מְבֹרָךְ מֵעַתָּה וְעַד עוֹלָם"

Let Hashem's name be blessed from now and forever.

3. LEADER CONTINUES:

"יְהִי שֵׁם ה' מְבֹרָךְ מֵעַתָּה וְעַד עוֹלָם"

Let Hashem's name be blessed from now and forever.

[If ten men join in the *zimun* add "אֱלֹקֵינוּ"]

"בִּרְשׁוּת מָרָנָן וְרַבָּנָן וְרַבּוֹתַי נְבָרֵךְ

[ten added: אֱלֹקֵינוּ] שֶׁאָכַלְנוּ מִשֶּׁלּוֹ"

With permission of our great teachers, Rabbis, and gentlemen who are here, let us bless [ten add: our G-d] the One, that we have eaten from what is His.

4. ALL RESPOND:

"בָּרוּךְ [ten add:אֱלֹקֵינוּ] שֶׁאָכַלְנוּ מִשֶּׁלּוֹ

וּבְטוּבוֹ חָיִינוּ"

Blessed is He, [ten add: our G-d] that we have eaten from what is His, and through His goodness we live.

9

הֶמְשֵׁךְ נוּסַח הַזִּימוּן
Bentching With a Group - Basic Text

The wording of the *Zimun* - continuation

ONE WHO HAS NOT EATEN WITH THE GROUP RESPONDS:

"בָּרוּךְ [אֱלֹקֵינוּ] :add ten] וּמְבֹרָךְ שְׁמוֹ תָּמִיד לְעוֹלָם וָעֶד"

Blessed is He, [ten add: our G-d] and His name is blessed continuously and forever.

5. LEADER REPEATS:

"בָּרוּךְ [אֱלֹקֵינוּ] :add ten] שֶׁאָכַלְנוּ מִשֶּׁלוֹ וּבְטוּבוֹ חָיִינוּ"

Blessed is He, [ten add: our G-d] that we have eaten from what is His, and through His goodness we live.

LEADER CONCLUDES:

"בָּרוּךְ הוּא וּבָרוּךְ שְׁמוֹ"
Blessed is He and blessed is His name.

The above is a basic outline of how to begin the *Birkas Hamazon*. By #3 of the outline, you may add different titles, right after the word *birshus*, depending on who is joining you in this *zimun*. When your father is at the table and you are leading the *bentching*, add *Avi, Mori* (my father, my teacher); for a great Sage, add *Moreinu veRabbeinu* (our teacher and our Rabbi); for your own teacher add *Mori veRabi* (my teacher and my Rabbi); for *Kohanim* add *Kohanim*; and when you are a guest say *Ba-al habayis hazeh*. Afterwards, you may continue with the words *Maranan veRabanan veRabosai.*

10

נוּסַח הַזִּימּוּן בְּשֶׁבַע בְּרָכוֹת
Bentching With a Group - *Sheva Berachos*

The wording of the *Zimun* for Sheva Berachos

A wedding is celebrated for seven days. To express our joy, we add this *zimun* - special prayer - to introduce *Birkas Hamazon*.

LEADER BEGINS:

"רבותי נברך"

Gentlemen, let us bentch.

ALL RESPOND:

"יהי שם ה' מברך מעתה ועד עולם"

Let Hashem's name be blessed from now and forever.

LEADER RESPONDS:

"יהי שם ה' מברך מעתה ועד עולם"

Let Hashem's name be blessed from now and forever.

LEADER CONTINUES:

"דוי הסר וגם חרון ואז אלם בשיר ירון
נחנו במעגלי צדק שעה ברכת בני ישורון
בני אהרן ברשות מרנן ורבנן ורבותי
נברך אלקינו שהשמחה במעונו ושאכלנו
משלו"

Remove pain and also anger, and then the mute (a person who was not able to speak) will sing

with joy. (In the World to Come, all handicaps will be healed.) Lead us in the ways of righteousness. Accept the blessing of the children of Jeshurun and the children of Aaron. With the permission of the great teachers, Rabbis, and gentlemen who are here, let us bless our G-d for the joy and that we have eaten from what is His.

ALL RESPOND:

"ברוך אלקינו שהשמחה במעונו ושאכלנו
משלו ובטובו חיינו"

Blessed is He, our G-d, for the joy and that we have eaten from what is His, and through His goodness we live.

LEADER REPEATS:

"ברוך אלקינו שהשמחה במעונו ושאכלנו
משלו ובטובו חיינו"

Blessed is He, our G-d, for the joy and that we have eaten from what is His, and through His goodness we live.

LEADER CONCLUDES:

"ברוך הוא וברוך שמו"

Blessed is He, and blessed is His name.

נוּסָח הַזִּימוּן בִּבְרִית מִילָה
Bentching With a Group - Bris Milah

The wording of the Zimun at a Bris Milah

At the *Birkas Hamazon* following a circumcision, we add the following introduction:

LEADER BEGINS:

"רבותי נברך"

Gentlemen, let us bentch.

ALL RESPOND:

"יהי שם ה' מברך מעתה ועד עולם"

Let Hashem's name be blessed from now and forever.

LEADER CONTINUES:

"יהי שם ה' מברך מעתה ועד עולם"

Let Hashem's name be blessed from now and forever.

"נודה לשמך בתוך אמוני ברוכים אתם לה'"

We give thanks to Your Name among the faithful ones. (The leader is speaking about the people who are seated and bentching with him. He calls them faithful because they have faith in Hashem.) You are blessed by Hashem.

"ברשות קל איום ונורא משגב לעתות בצרה קל נאזר בגבורה אדיר במרום ה'"

With permission of the fearful and awesome G-d, who is a tower of strength in times of trouble; Hashem who is all powerful, Hashem who is mighty in Heaven.

ALL RESPOND:

"נודה לשמך בתוך אמוני ברוכים אתם לה'"

We give thanks to Your Name among the faithful ones. You are blessed by Hashem.

LEADER:

"ברשות התורה הקדושה טהורה היא וגם פרושה צוה לנו מורשה משה עבד ה'"

With permission of the Torah which is holy, pure, and also clear, which was commanded to us as a tradition, by Moshe the servant of Hashem.

ALL RESPOND:

"נודה לשמך בתוך אמוני ברוכים אתם לה'"

We give thanks to Your Name among the faithful ones. You are blessed by Hashem.

The wording of the *Zimun* at a Bris Milah - continuation

LEADER:

"בִּרְשׁוּת הַכֹּהֲנִים וְהַלְוִיִּם אֶקְרָא לֵאלֹקֵי הָעִבְרִיִּים אוֹדֶנּוּ בְּכָל אִיִּים אֲבָרְכָה אֶת ה'"

With permission of the Kohanim, (and) the Levites, I will call to the G-d of the Hebrews, I will thank Him in all the islands, I will bless Hashem.

ALL RESPOND:

"נוֹדֶה לְשִׁמְךָ בְּתוֹךְ אֱמוּנֵי בְּרוּכִים אַתֶּם לַה'"

We give thanks to Your Name among the faithful ones. You are blessed by Hashem.

LEADER:

"בִּרְשׁוּת מָרָנָן וְרַבָּנָן וְרַבּוֹתַי אֶפְתַּח פִּי בְּשִׁיר וּשְׂפָתַי וְתֹאמַרְנָה עַצְמוֹתַי בָּרוּךְ הַבָּא בְּשֵׁם ה'"

With permission of my teachers and my Rabbis, I will open my mouth and lips with song, and my bones will say: Blessed is he who comes in the name of Hashem.

ALL RESPOND:

"נוֹדֶה לְשִׁמְךָ בְּתוֹךְ אֱמוּנֵי בְּרוּכִים אַתֶּם לַה'"

We give thanks to Your Name among the faithful ones. You are blessed by Hashem.

LEADER:

"בִּרְשׁוּת מָרָנָן וְרַבָּנָן וְרַבּוֹתַי נְבָרֵךְ [אֱלֹקֵינוּ] שֶׁאָכַלְנוּ מִשֶּׁלּוֹ"

With permission of our great teachers, Rabbis, and gentlemen who are here, let us bless [ten add: our G-d] that we have eaten from what is His.

ALL RESPOND:

"בָּרוּךְ [אֱלֹקֵינוּ] שֶׁאָכַלְנוּ מִשֶּׁלּוֹ וּבְטוּבוֹ חָיִינוּ"

Blessed is He [ten add: our G-d] that we have eaten from what is His and through His goodness we live.

LEADER:

"בָּרוּךְ [אֱלֹקֵינוּ] שֶׁאָכַלְנוּ מִשֶּׁלּוֹ וּבְטוּבוֹ חָיִינוּ"

Blessed is He [ten add: our G-d] that we have eaten from what is His and through His goodness we live.

ALL RESPOND:

"בָּרוּךְ הוּא וּבָרוּךְ שְׁמוֹ"

Blessed is He and blessed is His name.

19

הַמָּקוֹר לְבִרְכַּת הַמָּזוֹן

Source for *Birkas Hamazon*

The source for *Birkas Hamazon*

It is a positive commandment from the Torah to *bentch* the *Birkas Hamazon* after eating a meal with bread, as it is written, אלקיך 'ואכלת ושבעת וברכת את ה - And you should eat and be satisfied, then you should bless Hashem your G-d. Each of the words in this sentence of the Torah stands for a different part of *bentching*. Each blessing was set down at a different time in history.

1. "ברכת הזן" :"ואכלת"

In the desert, Hashem sent מן - food that came down from Heaven - for the Jews. At that time, Moshe decreed that this blessing be said. It begins with הזן את העולם - who nourishes the entire world, and ends with the words, הזן את הכל - thanking Hashem for giving food to everyone.

2. "ברכת הארץ" :"ושבעת"

After we entered *Eretz Yisrael*, Joshua instituted this additional blessing to be added to *Birkas Hamazon*. This blessing begins with נודה לך, and ends with -

על הארץ - thanking Hashem for giving us *Eretz Yisrael*.

3. "וברכת": "בונה ירושלים"

King David and King Solomon instituted another additional blessing. It begins with the words רחם - have mercy, and ends with, בונה ברחמיו ירושלים אמן - who builds Jerusalem in His mercy, Amen. In it we thank Hashem for Jerusalem and the *Beis Hamikdash*.

4. Immediately following the blessing בונה ירושלים - who builds Jerusalem, comes the *beracha*: הטוב והמטיב - who is good and does good.

The Rabbis decreed this blessing after what happened in the city of Beitar. There, the Romans killed many Jews and did not allow them to be buried. הטוב stands for the miracle which Hashem did for us, by not letting the bodies rot or even smell badly. המטיב thanks Hashem for allowing us to bury the dead later. (*Berachos* 48B)

14

בָּרוּךְ אַתָּה ה׳ אֱלֹקֵינוּ מֶלֶךְ הָעוֹלָם׳

Blessed are You Hashem

Blessed are You, Hashem, our G-d, King of the universe...

A person must be very careful to make a *beracha* with fear and great concentration. (*Chayei Adam Klal 5*) Try to understand what you are saying. (*Berachos 47*) Do not make a *beracha* out of habit, saying words without thinking about their meaning. This is a very serious sin. (*Mishnah Berurah 5:1*)

ברוך אתה ה׳ - **Boruch...Hashem.** The name of Hashem is written, *Yud - Kai - Vuv - Kai*: Have in mind

mind that Hashem is the master of all creation. He was; He is; He will be.

אלקינו - **Elohkeinu.** This name of G-d indicates that He is all powerful. There is nothing He cannot do. He is the master of all forces. (*Orach Chayim 5*) (These explanations are only concerning *berachos*. *Hashem Elohkeinu* has different meanings in other places.) The Vilna Gaon writes that the meaning of *Elohkeinu* is that Hashem Himself takes care of every single person. (*Aderes Eliyahu Devarim 6:4*)

15

הַזָּן אֶת הָעוֹלָם כֻּלּוֹ

Hashem Nourishes the Entire World

Medabeir

Chayos

Tzemach

Domein

Who "nourishes" the entire world...

Rabbeinu Bachya explains that the world can be divided into four parts:

1. *Domeim* - things that are not alive, such as rocks
2. *Tzemach* - things that grow, such as plants
3. *Chayos* - animals
4. *Medabeir* - those that speak, meaning human beings

1. How does Hashem "nourish" the *domeim*? Since the mountains and rocks do not need food, what does Hashem do to nourish them? By letting a mountain stay a mountain, or a valley remain a valley, Hashem is nourishing them. If at any time Hashem destroys them or allows them to decay, then Hashem is taking away their nourishment.

2. Plants are rooted. Hashem brings nourishment to them.

3. Animals can move, so they must search and hunt for food.

4. Man is above animals; he has the ability to think. Because man is able to, Hashem set up the world in such a way that man has to prepare the food he eats. Animals in contrast, eat their food as they find it. The amount a man needs to work in order to eat will depend on his trust in Hashem. The more a man has faith in Hashem, the less he will have to work to make a living. (*Kad HaKemach, Shaar HaParnassa*)

16

בְּטוּבוֹ בְּחֵן בְּחֶסֶד וּבְרַחֲמִים, הוּא נוֹתֵן לֶחֶם לְכָל בָּשָׂר,
כִּי לְעוֹלָם חַסְדּוֹ, וּבְטוּבוֹ הַגָּדוֹל"

All Good Things Come From Hashem

In His goodness, as a favor, with kindness, and with mercy, He gives bread to all flesh, both animals and people, because His kindness is endless. And in His great goodness...

"בטובו בחן בחסד וברחמים" - *in His goodness, as a favor, with kindness, and with mercy...*
It is man's nature to behave a certain way. He is jealous and stingy. This is not true of Hashem. Hashem always does good for us and is very generous to us. (*Etz Yosef*)

"הוא נותן לחם לכל בשר כי לעולם חסדו" - *He gives bread to all flesh, both animals and people, because His kindness is endless.*

This is taken from a *posuk* (verse) in *Tehillim* 136:25. Hashem has many different messengers to deliver His food. Sometimes it looks like *mazal* (luck), sometimes it looks like we are getting this food because we worked for it. However, it is important to remember that all this good comes from Hashem. He continually does kindness for us, without end. (*Malbim*)

"ובטובו הגדול" - *and in His great goodness...*
Hashem provides food to all people even when they are not deserving of His help. By saying these words, we are placing our faith in His great goodness. (*Iyun Tefillah*)

17

ענני כבוד

We never lacked, and may it be, that we will never lack "nourishment" - food. Why do we ask for this? So that we can praise Hashem, because He is the merciful One, who feeds and takes care of everyone, and who does good for everyone...

"תָּמִיד לֹא חָסַר לָנוּ" - *we never lacked...*

For forty years Hashem provided food for us in the desert. We never lacked anything. (*Nechemya* 9:21) All of our needs were completely taken care of by Hashem. (*Metzudas David*) We were always protected by the *ananei hakavod* - clouds which were above us in the desert. In addition, Hashem sent us food from the Heavens, gave us the well of Miriam so we would always have water, and our clothes grew with us and were always clean.

"וְאַל יֶחְסַר לָנוּ" - *and may we not lack...*

These words are actually a request to Hashem, "may we never be lacking." (*Yeshayahu* 51:14) While we are in *golus* - exile- our enemies surround us and try to destroy

us, but Hashem will not shame us. He will supply our needs. (*Radak*)

"בַּעֲבוּר שְׁמוֹ הַגָּדוֹל" - *for the sake of His Great Name...*

Hashem takes care of all that we need because of His great merciful name. (*Yaavetz*)

"כִּי הוּא אֵל זָן וּמְפַרְנֵס לַכֹּל וּמֵטִיב לַכֹּל" - *because He is the G-d who nourishes, supports, and does good for all...*

"זָן" - nourishes, refers to food

"וּמְפַרְנֵס" - supports, refers to clothing

"וּמֵטִיב" - does good, refers to shelter

These are the basic needs of life, and Hashem takes care of all of them for us. (*Etz Yosef*)

18

And He prepares food for all His creations which He has created...

While people are sleeping, Hashem stirs the winds, raises the clouds, brings rain to the earth, makes plants grow, dries them, and sets each person's table. (*Medrash Rabbah, Vayikra* 14:2) This *Medrash* is a proof that Hashem prepares ahead for all that we will need. (*Iyun Tefillah*)

19

בָּרוּךְ אַתָּה ה', הַזָּן אֶת הַכֹּל.
Blessed are You Hashem Who Nourishes All

Blessed are You, Hashem, who nourishes all.

"Everyone's eyes look to you with hope, and you give them their food in the proper time." (*Tehillim* 145:15) Hashem cares for people in many different ways. Some people receive the smallest amount that is needed, while some people receive much, much more than they need.

Hashem knows and cares for all of His creations. (*Malbim*) Before a person needs something, Hashem has already prepared for this time of need. (*Metzudas David*) The greatest proof that Hashem supplies all our needs is the fact that we have just eaten a meal. Who prepared this food for us? Hashem, of course.

We thank You, Hashem our G-d, that You have given the heritage of Eretz Yisrael to our forefathers, a land that is desired, which is good, and which is wide...

"נודה לך ח' אלקינו" - *We thank You, Hashem our G-d...*

This *beracha* does not begin with the words "Blessed are You...," to teach us that we should consider it attached to the first *beracha*. This follows the rule of *beracha hasmucha lechaverta* - a *beracha* which is next to its friend. When one long *beracha* begins with *Baruch ata...*, then the *beracha* which follows it does not begin with *Baruch*. (*Lavush*) "We thank You forever..." (*Tehillim* 79:13) - continually, every day of our lives. (*Malbim*)

"על שהנחלת לאבותינו" - *that You have given the heritage, Eretz Yisrael, to our forefathers...*

"He told His people of the power of His works, to give them the inheritance of the nations." (*Tehillim* 111:6) Why does the Torah begin with the story of Creation? So it should be clear to all that Hashem has complete power over the world. If the nations of the world accuse us of stealing *Eretz Yisrael* from the seven nations of Canaan, we will tell them, "*Eretz Yisrael* belongs to the Creator. The whole universe belongs to Hashem. It was His will to give it to you, and it was His will to take it back from you and give it to us." (*Rashi*)

"ארץ חמדה" - *a land that is desired...*

"And I give to you a desirable land, the finest inheritance." (*Yirmiyahu* 3:19)

Why is *Eretz Yisrael* called a desirable land?
1. The land itself is beautiful and pleasant.
2. It was given to us as an inheritance forever. (*Malbim*)
3. Although Hashem is everywhere, his Divine Presence is more easily felt in *Eretz Yisrael*, where the *Beis Hamikdash* was placed. (*Metzudas David*)

"טובה ורחבה" - *which is good and which is wide...*

"And I will bring them out of that land, to a land that is good and spacious." (*Shemos* 3:8) The *Ramban* explains that **good** means a land where the air itself is good and it is healthy for man. Every good thing is found in this land. The word **spacious** teaches us that there is plenty of room in the land for all of *Bnei Yisrael* to live there.

21

And that You took us out, Hashem our G-d, from the land of Egypt...

Why do we thank Hashem for taking "us" out of Egypt? Shouldn't we thank Hashem for taking "our fathers" out of Egypt? When speaking about *Eretz Yisrael*, we say that it is the inheritance of our fathers, but when talking about the going out of Egypt, each person in every generation should think of the redemption as a personal redemption. (*Pesachim* 115B) The *Ritvah* explains that when Hashem took the Jews out of Egypt, he redeemed all of Israel as one. This means that He not only took the Jews of that generation out of Egypt, but He also took out all future generations. Therefore, we should each look at ourselves as if Hashem had taken **us** out of Egypt, and we should thank and praise Hashem for doing this.

22

And saved us from the house of slavery...

"It was because of Hashem's love for you, and because He was keeping the promise that He made to your fathers, therefore, Hashem brought you out with a strong hand, setting you free from the house of slavery..." (*Devarim* 7:8) We did not deserve this great miracle. Still, Hashem took us out of Egypt because of His great love for us. He is waiting patiently for us to follow His commandments, so that we should be deserving of great reward. (*Daas Zekeinim*)

וְעַל בְּרִיתְךָ שֶׁחָתַמְתָּ בִּבְשָׂרֵנוּ

Giving the Commandment of Circumcision

And for the covenant which You sealed in our flesh...

Since women were not given the *mitzvah* of circumcision, there are opinions that women should not say these words in *bentching*. (*Rama - Orach Chayim* 187:3) However, the *Mishnah Berurah* 187:9 states, that women **should** mention the *bris*. They should thank Hashem for giving the commandment of circumcision to the men. It was as a reward for this *mitzvah* that *Eretz Yisrael* was given to all of us. The *Bedek Habayis* brings another reason that women should mention the *bris*. A person is not called *adam* - man - until he has a wife. Since a husband and wife become *basar echad* - one - women can mention the *bris* - circumcision.

וְעַל תּוֹרָתְךָ שֶׁלִּמַּדְתָּנוּ

Teaching us Torah

And for Your Torah which You taught us...

If not for the *bris* and the Torah, there would not longer be heaven and earth. If the earth would return to nothingness, we would never be given *Eretz Yisrael*. (*Etz Yosef*)

וְעַל חֻקֶּיךָ שֶׁחוֹדַעְתָּנוּ

Giving Us Rules to Follow

And for your statutes [laws] which You made known to us.

Why does it say "for the Torah which you **taught** us" and the "statutes which you **made known** to us"? What is the difference? "Torah" refers to laws which are logical. Because we can understand the reasoning behind them, Hashem taught them to us. "Statutes" are laws that man cannot understand, because it is Hashem's wisdom. These laws Hashem only "made known" to us. He did not teach us, but just told us the

rules. (*Iyun Tefillah*) One of the most famous examples of a *chok* (statute) is the *mitzvah* of *para adumah* (the red heifer). After slaughtering the red calf, its blood and ashes are used to purify someone who is *tamei* (spiritually impure). What makes it so strange is that the person who gets sprinkled these ashes becomes pure, while the person who does the sprinkling becomes *tamei*. Hashem wants us to learn the laws of the *para adumah* and do this *mitzvah*, even though we do not understand it.

26

And for life, grace, and the kindness which you do for us...

The *Iyun Tefillah* explains that life itself is a gift, and we should be thankful for it. Even if a person lives a life full of embarrassment and shame, he should still appreciate and thank Hashem for the gift of life. It is written in *Koheles* 9:4 that "a live dog is better than a dead lion." The Torah uses the word dog to describe something which has to do with shame, while the lion comes to show the strongest and mightiest of all animals. Even the lowest, living person can grow and improve, something which even the wisest, greatest dead person cannot do.

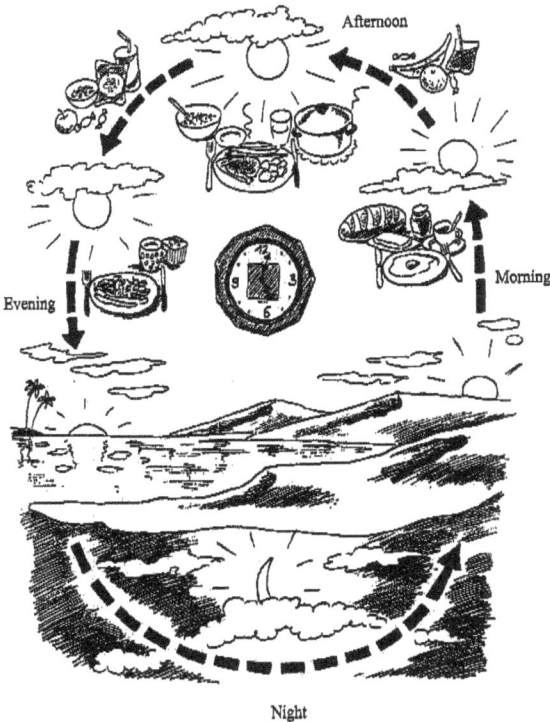

וְעַל אֲכִילַת מָזוֹן שָׁאַתָּה זָן וּמְפַרְנֵס אוֹתָנוּ תָּמִיד,
בְּכָל יוֹם וּבְכָל עֵת וּבְכָל שָׁעָה.

Realizing that Hashem Provides Each Day's Needs

Afternoon

Morning

Evening

Night

And for eating of the food with which You nourish us, and which You provide for us constantly every day, and at set times of the day, and in every hour.

In *tefilas shacharis* - the morning prayers, we praise Hashem by saying, "And in His goodness, each day He continues to renew the work of creation." Hashem gives life. It is He who causes something to exist - to be or not to be. If Hashem would hold back His goodness for even one second, the whole world would return to nothingness. (*Etz Yosef*)

"בכל יום ובכל עת ובכל שעה" - *every day, and at set times of the day, and in every hour*

Every day - The *Mishnah Berurah* 157:4 quotes the *Zohar, Parshas Beshalach*, "One should not cook on one day for the next day, or leave over food from one day to the next." Instead, a person should look to Hashem each day and *daven* to Him for food. In this way, Hashem will bless him each day.

At set times - This is referring to the three regular mealtimes of the day: morning, afternoon, and evening.

Every hour - This is referring to even those times when a person does not usually eat. (*Iyun Tefillah*)

וְעַל מַסִּים וְעַל הַפָּרְקָן וְעַל הַגְּבוּרוֹת וְעַל הַתְּשׁוּעוֹת וְעַל הַמִּלְחָמוֹת שֶׁעָשִׂיתָ לַאֲבוֹתֵינוּ בַּיָּמִים הָהֵם בַּזְּמַן הַזֶּה:

בִּימֵי מַתִּתְיָהוּ בֶּן יוֹחָנָן כֹּהֵן גָּדוֹל חַשְׁמוֹנָאִי וּבָנָיו, כְּשֶׁעָמְדָה מַלְכוּת יָוָן הָרְשָׁעָה עַל עַמְּךָ יִשְׂרָאֵל, לְהַשְׁכִּיחָם תּוֹרָתֶךָ, וּלְהַעֲבִירָם מֵחֻקֵּי רְצוֹנֶךָ. וְאַתָּה בְּרַחֲמֶיךָ הָרַבִּים, עָמַדְתָּ לָהֶם בְּעֵת צָרָתָם, רַבְתָּ אֶת רִיבָם, דַּנְתָּ אֶת דִּינָם, נָקַמְתָּ אֶת נִקְמָתָם. מָסַרְתָּ גִבּוֹרִים בְּיַד חַלָּשִׁים, וְרַבִּים בְּיַד מְעַטִּים, וּטְמֵאִים בְּיַד טְהוֹרִים, וּרְשָׁעִים בְּיַד צַדִּיקִים, וְזֵדִים בְּיַד עוֹסְקֵי תוֹרָתֶךָ. וּלְךָ עָשִׂיתָ שֵׁם גָּדוֹל וְקָדוֹשׁ בְּעוֹלָמֶךָ, וּלְעַמְּךָ יִשְׂרָאֵל עָשִׂיתָ תְּשׁוּעָה גְדוֹלָה וּפֻרְקָן כְּהַיּוֹם הַזֶּה. וְאַחַר כֵּן בָּאוּ בָנֶיךָ לִדְבִיר בֵּיתֶךָ, וּפִנּוּ אֶת הֵיכָלֶךָ, וְטִהֲרוּ אֶת מִקְדָּשֶׁךָ, וְהִדְלִיקוּ נֵרוֹת בְּחַצְרוֹת קָדְשֶׁךָ, וְקָבְעוּ שְׁמוֹנַת יְמֵי חֲנֻכָּה אֵלּוּ, לְהוֹדוֹת וּלְהַלֵּל לְשִׁמְךָ הַגָּדוֹל.

Prayer of Thanks for the Miracles of Chanukah

For the miracles - for **Chanukah:** *In the days of Mattisyahu the son of Yonachan the High Priest, the* Hasmonean *and his sons...*

During Chanukah and Purim we add the *beracha Al Hanissim* (for the miracles). Since *Al Hanissim* is a prayer of thanks for the miracles of Chanukah and Purim, we include it in *Birkas Ha-aretz* (which begins with *Nodeh*), which is also a prayer of thanks.

For Chanukah and Purim add: "We thank You for the miracles, for freeing us to serve Hashem, for the mighty acts, for saving us, and for wars (that You fought for us), - that You did for our fathers in those days at this time."

Each and every day, Hashem does miracles for us just as He did for our forefathers. Some are easy for us to see, while some are not. (*Lavush*)

CHANUKAH
"In the days of Mattisyahu the son of Yochanan, the Kohein Gadol *(the High Priest), the* Hasmonean *and*

his sons, the wicked kingdom of Greece ruled over Your nation Yisroel, to make them forget Your Torah, and to lead them away from Your mitzvos. You, in Your great kindness, stood by them in their time of trouble. You fought their fights; judged their judgments; took revenge for them. You handed the strong to the weak. You let a few people conquer many people. You handed those who are tamei into the hands of those who are tahor. You made the wicked people lose to the righteous people. You handed people who did sins to people who keep Your Torah. For Yourself, You made a great and holy name in Your world. On this day, You saved and freed us. Afterwards, Your children came to the holiest place of Your house, and they cleaned out Your Beis Hamikdash (Temple). They lit lights in the courtyard of Your Beis Hamikdash, and they set down for all time that these eight days of Chanukah should be used for giving thanks and praises to Your great name."

29

וְעַל הַנִּסִּים וְעַל הַפֻּרְקָן וְעַל הַגְּבוּרוֹת וְעַל הַתְּשׁוּעוֹת וְעַל הַמִּלְחָמוֹת שֶׁעָשִׂיתָ לַאֲבוֹתֵינוּ בַּיָּמִים הָהֵם בַּזְּמַן הַזֶּה:

בִּימֵי מָרְדְּכַי וְאֶסְתֵּר בְּשׁוּשַׁן הַבִּירָה, כְּשֶׁעָמַד עֲלֵיהֶם הָמָן הָרָשָׁע, בִּקֵּשׁ לְהַשְׁמִיד לַהֲרוֹג וּלְאַבֵּד אֶת כָּל הַיְּהוּדִים, מִנַּעַר וְעַד זָקֵן, טַף וְנָשִׁים בְּיוֹם אֶחָד, בִּשְׁלוֹשָׁה עָשָׂר לְחֹדֶשׁ שְׁנֵים עָשָׂר, הוּא חֹדֶשׁ אֲדָר, וּשְׁלָלָם לָבוֹז. וְאַתָּה בְּרַחֲמֶיךָ הָרַבִּים הֵפַרְתָּ אֶת עֲצָתוֹ, וְקִלְקַלְתָּ אֶת מַחֲשַׁבְתּוֹ, וַהֲשֵׁבוֹתָ לּוֹ גְּמוּלוֹ בְּרֹאשׁוֹ, וְתָלוּ אוֹתוֹ וְאֶת בָּנָיו עַל הָעֵץ.

Prayer of Thanks for the Miracles of Purim

For the miracles - for **Purim:** *In the days of Mordechai and Esther, in the capital of Shushan...*

PURIM

"In the days of Mordechai and Esther, in the capital of Shushan, when the wicked Haman stood up against them (the Jewish people), he wanted to destroy, to kill, and to wipe out all the Jewish people, infants and women, on one day, (that is), on the thirteenth day of the twelfth month, which is the month of Adar. But You, in Your great kindness, caused this bad advice to fail, and did not allow his evil ideas to happen. You caused all his plans to backfire. They hanged him and his sons on the gallows."

30

וְעַל הַכֹּל ה׳ אֱלֹקֵינוּ אֲנַחְנוּ מוֹדִים לָךְ,
וּמְבָרְכִים אוֹתָךְ, יִתְבָּרַךְ שִׁמְךָ בְּפִי כָּל חַי תָּמִיד לְעוֹלָם וָעֶד.
Thanking Hashem for Everything

And for everything, Hashem our G-d, we thank You, and bless You, may Your name be blessed in the mouth of all living creatures, always, for all time.

"וְעַל הכל ה׳ אלקינו אנחנו מודים לך ומברכים אותך" - *And for everything, Hashem our G-d, we thank You, and bless You*

V'al hakol is part of the beracha called Birkas Ha-aretz. The beracha begins with Nodeh (we thank Hashem), and ends with v'al hakol (on everything we thank You), to teach us that a person should give praise and thanks

at the beginning and the end. (*Berachos 49A*) By talking about all the things Hashem has done for us, it brings us to a greater appreciation, so we thank Him again. (*Etz Yosef*)

"יתברך שמך בפי כל חי תמיד לעולם ועד" - *May Your name be blessed in the mouth of all living creatures, always, for all time.*

Right now only Jews praise Hashem. So we ask Hashem to send *Moshiach*, when everyone will recognize that Hashem is the One and Only. Then everyone will praise and serve Hashem. (*Etz Yosef*)

31

כַּכָּתוּב, וְאָכַלְתָּ וְשָׂבָעְתָּ, וּבֵרַכְתָּ אֶת ה'
אֱלֹקֶיךָ, עַל הָאָרֶץ הַטֹּבָה אֲשֶׁר נָתַן לָךְ.

Looking for Ways to Bring Greater Honor to Hashem's Name

„וְאָכַלְתָּ..

..וְשָׂבָעְתָּ...

...וּבֵרַכְתָּ."

For it is written: "And you should eat, and be satisfied, and bless Hashem, Your G-d, for the good land which He gave you."

Hashem said to the angels, "I cannot turn away from my *Bnei Yisrael*. I wrote in the Torah, 'you should eat, and be satisfied, and bless your G-d.' The Torah only demands that a person *bentch* after he is satisfied and full, but My people so much want to thank Hashem for what He gives them that they are very careful with the measurements of bread. They *bentch* on even the smallest amount that could satisfy a person - which is a *kezayis*."

The *mitzvah* of *Birkas Hamazon* is written in the singular form, *v'achalta* - and you should eat. However, the Jewish people, who are always looking for ways to honor Hashem's name, run to form a *zimun* - a group of three or more men. If a person sees that he has a meal of bread, but does not have a *zimun* with whom to *bentch*, he will look to share his food with others so he can *bentch* with a group and bring greater praise to Hashem's name.

בָּרוּךְ אַתָּה חי, עַל הָאָרֶץ וְעַל הַמָּזוֹן.

Thanking Hashem for the Land and for the Food

Blessed are You, Hashem, for the land and for the food.

Even though this blessing talks about two things, the land and the food, it is really one *beracha*. We bless Hashem who gave us the land which produces food. (*Berachos* 49A) When we say this *beracha*, we should also keep in mind the food which Hashem has just given us. (*Etz Yosef*)

33

Have mercy, Hashem our G-d, on us and on Israel, Your people, and on Jerusalem, Your city...

"רחם ה' אלקינו, עלינו ועל ישראל עמך" - *Have mercy, Hashem our G-d, on us and on Israel, Your people*

Just as a father has mercy on his children, please, Hashem, have mercy on us. (*Etz Yosef*)

From this point on in the *Birkas Hamazon*, we ask Hashem for things which are similar to our prayers in the *Shemoneh Esreh*. *Rachem*, is like the tenth blessing in *Shemoneh Esreh*, which is *Tekah Beshofar* - (Sound

the great shofar). We *daven* to Hashem that He should gather together all of those in exile. (*Iyun Tefillah*)

"ועל ירושלים עירך" - *and on Jerusalem, Your city*

This can be compared to the fourteenth *beracha* of *Shemoneh Esreh* which begins with the words, *Tishkon besoch Yerushalayim ircha* (may Your *Shechina* be found in Jerusalem, Your city). (*Iyun Tefillah*) Hashem says, "I will return to Zion and stay in Jerusalem." (*Zecharyah* 8:3) Jerusalem is the capital of Hashem's kingdom, and the *Beis Hamikdash* was built there. (*Radak*)

34

וְעַל צִיּוֹן מִשְׁכַּן כְּבוֹדֶךָ, וְעַל מַלְכוּת בֵּית דָּוִד מְשִׁיחֶךָ, וְעַל הַבַּיִת הַגָּדוֹל וְהַקָּדוֹשׁ שֶׁנִּקְרָא שִׁמְךָ עָלָיו.

Remembering Jerusalem, the Kingdom of David, and the Beis Hamikdash

And on Zion, the place of Your honor, and on the kingdom of the house of David, Your anointed one, and on the Holy **Beis Hamikdash**, *which is called by Your name.*

"וְעַל צִיּוֹן מִשְׁכַּן כְּבוֹדֶךָ" - *and on Zion, the place of Your honor*

Zion here means Jerusalem. "If I forget Jerusalem, let my right hand become useless. Let my tongue stick to the roof of my mouth." (*Tehillim* 137:5,6) *Chazal* gave us different ways to remember the destruction of Jerusalem. When plastering a house, a person would leave a part of the wall un-plastered. Certain foods were not eaten, and certain jewelry was not worn to remind us of the destruction. (*Baba Basra* 60B) The *Maharsha* explains that after completing a meal, a person should sit at his table a little longer without eating. This is to remember that our beloved *Beis Hamikdash* was destroyed.

"וְעַל מַלְכוּת בֵּית דָּוִד מְשִׁיחֶךָ" - *and on the kingdom of the house of David, Your anointed one...*

This *beracha* is like the seventeenth *beracha* of *Shemoneh Esreh*, which speaks about our waiting for Hashem to return to Jerusalem and to build the third *Beis Hamikdash*. This final *Beis Hamikdash* will be greater than the earlier ones. (*Haggai* 2:9) We know that the second *Beis Hamikdash* was destroyed because there was *sinas chinam* (groundless hatred), a time when Jews were not getting along with one another. The *Malbim* explains that the third *Beis Hamikdash* will not be destroyed, as there will not be hatred between brothers.

אֱלֹקֵינוּ אָבִינוּ רְעֵנוּ זוּנֵנוּ פַּרְנְסֵנוּ וְכַלְכְּלֵנוּ וְהַרְוִיחֵנוּ,

Asking Hashem to Continue to Take Care of Us

Our, G-d, Our Father, watch over us, feed us, give us clothing and a place to live, support us regularly, and give us enough to live comfortably...

When we speak about the things Hashem does for us, it reminds us that even though we have gone through difficult times since the *Beis Hamikdash* was destroyed, Hashem always takes care of us. (*Iyun Tefillah*)

וְהָרַוח לָנוּ ה׳ אֱלֹקֵינוּ מְהֵרָה מִכָּל צָרוֹתֵינוּ.

Praying for Relief From Our Troubles

Quickly give us relief Hashem, our G-d from all of our troubles

"Hashem, save Yisrael from all of its troubles." (*Tehillim* 25:22) King David says, "I am praying not only for myself, but for the sake of all of Israel." (*Metsudas David*) He asks that his prayers should be accepted for everyone. This is the way a *sheliach tsibur davens*.

וְנָא אַל תַּצְרִיכֵנוּ ה' אֱלֹקֵינוּ, לֹא לִידֵי מַתְּנַת בָּשָׂר וָדָם, וְלֹא לִידֵי הַלְוָאָתָם

Praying that We Should Not Need to Depend on People

And please, Hashem our G-d, do not let us need the gifts of people or their loans...

"I will not take anything that is yours, not a thread or a shoelace. You should not be able to say, 'It was I who made Avram rich.'" (*Bereishis* 14:23) Hashem had promised Avraham *Avinu* that He would make him wealthy, and Avraham had full trust in Hashem. (*Rashi*)

If Avraham accepted anything from the King of Sedom, people would say that it was the King of Sedom who made Avraham rich. To make it clear that the blessing came from Hashem and not the King of Sedom, Avraham did not take even the smallest thing from the King. He did not want to take away from the honor of Hashem. (*Gur Aryeh*)

38

But only of Your hand, which is full, open, holy, and generous...

"When you eat by the work of your hands, you will be happy (in this world), and it will be good for you (in the next world)." (*Tehillim* 128:2) When a person supports himself by his own work, then he alone gets the full reward for his Torah learning. (*Metzudas David*)

Asking Hashem to Protect Us From Embarrassment and Shame

That he should not be embarrassed or ashamed forever.

Our Rabbis taught us that there are three things which cause a person to do things he knows are wrong, and to go against Hashem's will.

1. Idol worshipers pressuring a person to go against the Torah.

2. An evil spirit making a person insane.

3. Being poor. (*Eruvin* 41B)

A person can choose to do certain *mitzvos*, but there are other *mitzvos* which **must** be done. Sometimes a person cannot do certain *mitzvos*, for example, because he does not have the money needed.

As a result, he feels embarrassed in **this** world. However, when it comes to a *mitzvah* that we **must** do (such as learning Torah, or honoring our parents), a person who does not do them will be ashamed in the **next** world. (*Etz Yosef*) So we ask Hashem to protect us. Do not let us become embarrassed, and certainly, do not let us become ashamed.

On weekdays turn to page 47; on Shabbos turn to page 41; on Yom Tov, Chol Hamoed and Rosh Chodesh turn to page 45.

רְצֵה וְהַחֲלִיצֵנוּ ה' אֱלֹקֵינוּ בְּמִצְוֹתֶיךָ, וּבְמִצְוַת יוֹם הַשְּׁבִיעִי הַשַּׁבָּת הַגָּדוֹל וְהַקָּדוֹשׁ הַזֶּה

Special Shabbos Prayer

This prayer is added on Shabbos

Retzei is a prayer for Hashem's mercy. We add it here, in the blessing of *Boneh Yerushalayim*, since they are both prayers for Hashem's mercy. (*Mishnah Berurah* 188:12)

Be pleased and save us, Hashem our G-d, by Your commandments and by the mitzvah of the seventh day - which is the mitzvah of keeping Shabbos

Rabbi Eliezer ben Yaakov said, the word *v'hahalitsaynu* has many meanings. It is a prayer to "loosen," or ease our suffering; "give us a place to hide" from all of our troubles; give us the "weapons," or the ability to overcome our difficulties; and allow us "to rest" and not to have to worry about making a living. (*Talmud Yerushalmi Shabbos*) As a reward for keeping the laws of Shabbos properly, we ask Hashem to take us out of *Golus*, and let us come back to *Eretz Yisrael* and be strong. (*Etz Yosef*)

41

כִּי יוֹם זֶה גָּדוֹל וְקָדוֹשׁ הוּא לְפָנֶיךָ, לִשְׁבָּת בּוֹ וְלָנוּחַ בּוֹ בְּאַהֲבָה כְּמִצְוַת רְצוֹנֶךָ,

Shabbos is a Special Day, a Holy Day and a Day of Complete Rest While Keeping the Commandment of Shabbos

Because this is a great day before You to rest and be calm on it, with love, as a commandment of your will.

Shabbos is a special day. It is a time for a person to stop and think. Rashi explains that "rest" in the Torah means not only rest from physical work, but also rest from thinking about the worries of the week. The Shabbos allows us to elevate our entire being to be close to Hashem. Through being in the company of family and

great people, a person leaves his day to day life and embraces the holiness and tranquility that only a Shabbos can give. Just as Hashem created the world in six days and rested on the seventh, so do we rest as beloved children in Hashem's holy presence.

Learning together and enjoying the true *ruach* (spirit) of Shabbos, along with tasting the delights (fruits, candies, etc) that come with it, fulfill the will of Hashem.

42

וּבִרְצוֹנְךָ הָנִיחַ לָנוּ ה׳ אֱלֹקֵינוּ, שֶׁלֹּא תְהֵא צָרָה וְיָגוֹן וַאֲנָחָה בְּיוֹם מְנוּחָתֵנוּ,

Protect Us From Harm On Our Day of Rest

Let it be Your will to allow us to rest, Hashem our G-d, so that there will be no trouble, or sadness, or moaning on our day of rest.

Because You chose this day as a day of rest, we ask that You should not let anything happen that would cause us to break the laws of Shabbos. (*Etz Yosef*)

Through observing the laws properly, the "fence" of Shabbos protects us from life and death situations. The outside world, in contrast, does not have the safeguard Shabbos.

וְהַרְאֵנוּ ה' אֱלֹקֵינוּ בְּנֶחָמַת צִיּוֹן עִירֶךָ, וּבְבִנְיַן יְרוּשָׁלַיִם עִיר קָדְשֶׁךָ, כִּי אַתָּה הוּא בַּעַל הַיְשׁוּעוֹת וּבַעַל הַנֶּחָמוֹת.

Allow Us to Rebuild the Beis Hamikdash and Serve Hashem

And let us see, Hashem our G-d, Zion Your city being comforted, and Jerusalem, the city of Your holiness, being rebuilt, because You are the One who has power to help and the ability to give comfort.

"וְהַרְאֵנוּ... בְּנֶחָמַת צִיּוֹן עִירֶךָ וּבְבִנְיַן יְרוּשָׁלַיִם עִיר קָדְשֶׁךָ" - *And let us see, Hashem our G-d, Zion Your city being comforted, and Jerusalem, the city of Your holiness, being rebuilt...*

"Because Hashem comforted Zion" (*Yeshayahu* 51:3) Hashem will comfort Zion in the future, yet the Prophet uses the past tense, as if Zion has been comforted. Since we have complete trust that Hashem is going to take us out of exile, it is written as if He already did it. (*Metsudos David*)

"כִּי אַתָּה הוּא בַּעַל הַיְשׁוּעוֹת וּבַעַל הַנֶּחָמוֹת" - *because You are the One who has the power to help and the ability to give comfort*

"I am, I am, He that comforts you." (*Yeshayahu* 51:12) When Hashem comforts a person, it is a true comfort. (*Metsudas David*)

On Yom Tov, Chol Hamoed and Rosh Chodesh turn to page 45. Every other Shabbos turn to page 47

אֱלֹקֵינוּ וֵאלֹקֵי אֲבוֹתֵינוּ, יַעֲלֶה, וְיָבֹא, וְיַגִּיעַ, וְיֵרָאֶה, וְיֵרָצֶה, וְיִשָּׁמַע,
וְיִפָּקֵד, וְיִזָּכֵר זִכְרוֹנֵנוּ וּפִקְדוֹנֵנוּ, וְזִכְרוֹן אֲבוֹתֵינוּ, וְזִכְרוֹן מָשִׁיחַ בֶּן דָּוִד
עַבְדֶּךָ, וְזִכְרוֹן יְרוּשָׁלַיִם עִיר קָדְשֶׁךָ, וְזִכְרוֹן כָּל עַמְּךָ בֵּית יִשְׂרָאֵל
לְפָנֶיךָ, לִפְלֵיטָה לְטוֹבָה לְחֵן וּלְחֶסֶד וּלְרַחֲמִים, לְחַיִּים וּלְשָׁלוֹם בְּיוֹם:

Rosh Chodesh : רֹאשׁ הַחֹדֶשׁ הַזֶּה.

Passover : חַג הַמַּצּוֹת הַזֶּה.

Shavuos : חַג הַשָּׁבוּעוֹת הַזֶּה.

Sukkos : חַג הַסֻּכּוֹת הַזֶּה.

Shemini Atzeres and Simchas Torah : שְׁמִינִי חַג הָעֲצֶרֶת הַזֶּה.

Rosh Hashanah : הַזִּכָּרוֹן הַזֶּה.

Prayer Added on the New Moon, New Year, and Festivals

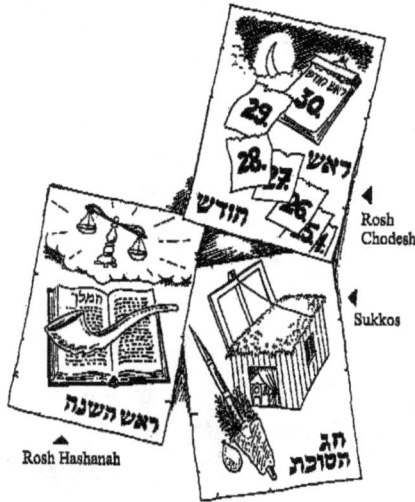

Rosh
Chodesh

Sukkos

Rosh Hashanah

חג השבועות

ראש השנה

חג הסכות

Rise and come up

Our G-d and the G-d of our fathers, let (our pleas) go up, and come (to You), and reach (You), and be seen (by You), and be accepted, and be heard, and be counted, and be remembered, a reminder and thoughts of us, and a reminder of our forefathers, a reminder of Jerusalem, Your city, and a reminder of Moshiah, the son of David, Your servant, and a reminder of all Your people, the House of Israel, (should come) before You. (Think of us) to save us, for our good, as a favor, and as a kindness, and with mercy, for a good life, and for peace, on this day of:

ראש החדש	*Rosh Chodesh (the New Month)*
חג המצות	*the Festival of Matzos*

חג השבעות	*the Festival of Shavuos*
הזכרון	*Remembrance (on Rosh Hashana)*
חג הסכות	*the Festival of Sukkos*
וחג שמיני עצרת	*the Festival of Shemini Atzeres (and Simchas Torah)*

To have mercy on us on this day and to save us. Remember us, Hashem our G-d, on this day, for good, and think of us for blessing, and save us for a good life. And having to do with saving and mercy, have pity on us and show us favor, and have compassion and mercy on us and save us. Because our eyes (look) to You, because You are G-d, King, kind and merciful.

זָכְרֵנוּ ה' אֱלֹקֵינוּ בּוֹ לְטוֹבָה, וּפָקְדֵנוּ בּוֹ לִבְרָכָה, וְהוֹשִׁיעֵנוּ בּוֹ לְחַיִּים. וּבִדְבַר יְשׁוּעָה וְרַחֲמִים, חוּס וְחָנֵּנוּ וְרַחֵם עָלֵינוּ וְהוֹשִׁיעֵנוּ, כִּי אֵלֶיךָ עֵינֵינוּ, כִּי קֵל מֶלֶךְ חַנּוּן וְרַחוּם אָתָּה.

Prayer Added on the New Moon, New Year, and Festivals

1. זכרון ירושלים

2. משיח בן דוד

3. תחיית המתים

4. עקידת יצחק

5. קרבנות בבית המקדש

6. תורה

7. יציאת מצרים

8. אבות הקדושים

Rise up and come

This is a prayer for Hashem's mercy. We add it here, in the blessing of *Boneh Yerushalayim*, since they are both prayers for Hashem's mercy. (*Mishnah Berurah* 188:12)

Ya'aleh Veyavo uses eight words, one after another, to ask Hashem to remember us and to consider our needs. These words stand for the eight levels that separate man from Hashem. Because we sinned, Hashem moved further away from earth. We pray that our remembrance should rise above these levels, and be brought right in front of Hashem. (*Iyun Tefillah*)

The Vilna Gaon explains that these eight requests stand for something far deeper. They are:
1. "Let it rise up" - remember Jerusalem (*Tehillim* 137:6)
2. "and come to You" - remember *Moshiach* (*Zecharyah* 3:8)

3. "and reach You" - remember that Hashem will bring the dead back to life (*Daniel* 12:12)
4. "and be seen" - remember *Akedas Yitzchak*, the binding of Isaac on the altar (*Bereishis* 22:14)
5. "and be accepted" - remember the sacrifices we brought in the *Beis Hamikdash* (*Yeshayahu* 56:7)
6. "and be heard" - remember the study of the Torah (*Malachi* 3:16)
7. "and think about" - remember how You took us out of Egypt (*Shemos* 3:16)
8. "and remember" - remember the agreement You made with our forefathers (*Vayikra* 26:45)

The order of the requests is also important. Let the thought of us go up to Heaven, and come to Your holy place, and reach its proper place, and be seen in front of You, and be accepted for good, so that the whole world will hear that Hashem has thought about His decree and remembers His agreement and His promise to save His people. (*Iyun Tefillah*)

וּבְנֵה יְרוּשָׁלַיִם עִיר הַקֹּדֶשׁ בִּמְהֵרָה בְיָמֵינוּ. בָּרוּךְ אַתָּה ה' בּוֹנֵה בְּרַחֲמָיו יְרוּשָׁלָיִם. אָמֵן.

Rebuild Your Holy City, Jerusalem

And may You build Jerusalem, the holy city, quickly, in our days. Blessed are You, Hashem, who builds Jerusalem. Amen

"Hashem is the builder of Jerusalem; He will gather together those Jews that were thrown out of Eretz Yisrael [when it was destroyed]." (*Tehillim* 147:2) Hashem Himself will rebuild Jerusalem. It will be a holy city, and everyone will be able to feel that Hashem is there. (*Malbim*)

אָמֵן - *Amen*

This is the end of the third blessing. It can be read in two ways, either as:

1. a prayer, or
2. a way of saying thank you.

As a prayer: May Jerusalem be rebuilt quickly, during our life time. As an expression of thanks: We give thanks to You, Your name is blessed, that You will surely rebuild Jerusalem.

47

בָּרוּךְ אַתָּה ה' אֱלֹקֵינוּ מֶלֶךְ הָעוֹלָם, הָקֵל אָבִינוּ מַלְכֵּנוּ אַדִּירֵנוּ
בּוֹרְאֵנוּ גּוֹאֲלֵנוּ יוֹצְרֵנוּ קְדוֹשֵׁנוּ קְדוֹשׁ יַעֲקֹב:

Hashem, Our Father, Our Powerful King, Our Creator and Protector

מלך משפט

אב הרחמן

Blessed are You, Hashem our G-d, King of the universe, the Almighty, our Father, our King, our Strong One, our Creator, our Redeemer, our Maker, our Holy One, the Holy One of Yaakov.

This, the fourth *beracha* of *Birkas Hamazon* is not a Torah requirement as are the first three *berachos*. This *beracha* does not end with *baruch* (blessing), to emphasize that this is a rabbinical requirement and not a Torah blessing.

"הָקֵל אָבִינוּ" - *The Almighty, our Father* - Whenever we are in trouble, we can always turn to you. Hashem is the only one who can help us. (*Malbim*)

"מַלְכֵּנוּ" - *Our King* - "For Hashem is our judge; Hashem is the one who gave us our laws; Hashem is our King; He will save us." (*Yeshayahu* 33:22)

"אַדִּירֵנוּ" - *Our strong one* - Since Hashem is strong, He will be able to overpower any enemy, no matter how strong or large. (*Metzudas David*).

"בּוֹרְאֵנוּ" - *Our Creator* - When we do *mitzvos*, we should understand that we were created so we can do Hashem's commandments. That is our reason for living.

"גּוֹאֲלֵנוּ" - *The one who takes us out of exile* - "Your name is forever." (*Yeshayahu* 63:16) Everyone knows You by the name of "Father and the One who saves Israel." (*Malbim*)

"בּוֹרְאֵנוּ" - *Our Maker* - "We are the clay and you are the potter." (*Yeshayahu*) Hashem shapes the behavior of his people through *mussar*.

"קְדוֹשֵׁנוּ קְדוֹשׁ יַעֲקֹב" - *Our Holy One, the Holy One of Yaakov* - When a man does something which makes other people realize the greatness of Hashem, this is done *al kiddush Hashem*. As a result of this person's holy actions, other people come to praise Hashem. (*Malbim*)

48

רוֹעֵנוּ רוֹעֵה יִשְׂרָאֵל,
הַמֶּלֶךְ הַטּוֹב וְהַמֵּטִיב לַכֹּל

Hashem, Our Shepherd

Our shepherd, the sheperd of Israel, the King who is good and who does good to all.

"רוֹעֵנוּ" - *Our shepherd*

"Hashem is my Shepherd, I will not lack anything." (*Tehillim* 23:1) King David feels that since Hashem has the power to do anything, there is no need to worry. Like a shepherd, Hashem will take care of all our needs. (*Metzudas David*)

"רועה ישראל" - *the shepherd of Israel*

We are used to thinking that when Hashem does miracles such as saving us from an enemy, this is a great wonder. Rav Yochanan, however, teaches us that the fact that Hashem takes care of our day-to-day needs is even more extraordinary. Taking us out of exile is carried out by an angel, as it says, "the angel who redeemed me from all evil." (*Bereishis* 48:16) But Hashem Himself takes care of our day to day needs, "as a shepherd..." (*Bereishis* 48:15) Hashem takes care of our needs, like a shepherd who watches over each of his animals. (*Pesachim* 118A)

"המלך הטוב והמטיב לכל" - *the king who is good and who does good to all*

"You are good and You do good." (*Tehillim* 119:68) *Hatov*: You are good to us without our even asking for Your goodness. *Hameitiv*: When we pray for help, You answer by doing good for us. (*Metzudas David*)

49

שֶׁבְּכָל יוֹם וָיוֹם

Trust in Hashem Each Day

That each and every day

Rav Elazar Hagadol said, "The person who has bread in his basket but asks, 'What will I eat tomorrow?' does not have a strong belief in Hashem." (*Sotah* 48B) When Hashem creates a day, He also creates each of the things which a person will need for that day. So a person should not worry about tomorrow. If he trusts in Hashem, Hashem will take care of his needs. (*Etz Yosef*)

Trust in Hashem: Thanks for the Past, Present, and Future

He did good; He does good; He will do good for us. He did kindness TO us; He does kindness for us: He will do kindness for us forever.

This *beracha* was written by Rabban Gamliel the Elder to express *hakoras hatov* (gratitude) for the miracle that Hashem did for those killed in Beitar.

When Rome ruled over the Jewish nation, Bar Kochba led the Jews of Beitar and rebelled against the enemy. The Romans beat the Jewish army and killed hundreds of thousands of men, women, and children.

When the Jews wanted to bury the dead bodies, the Romans would not allow it. For years the dead were left unburied in the open fields of Beitar. Rabban Gamliel and his court fasted and *davened* for many days. Rabban Gamliel then sent a huge bribe to the Romans before they gave the Jews permission to bury the dead people.

The miracle was that the bodies did not smell or rot. They were fresh and whole.

The Rabbinical court set down this blessing for future generations. It thanks Hashem for His double goodness - "hatov," for keeping the bodies fresh, and "hametiv," for allowing us to bury them.

לְחֵן וּלְחֶסֶד וּלְרַחֲמִים וּלְרֶוַח הַצָּלָה וְהַצְלָחָה, בְּרָכָה וִישׁוּעָה
נֶחָמָה פַּרְנָסָה וְכַלְכָּלָה וְרַחֲמִים וְחַיִּים וְשָׁלוֹם וְכָל טוֹב, וּמִכָּל טוּב
לְעוֹלָם אַל יְחַסְּרֵנוּ:

Prayer That We Should Never Have Too Little

1. לְחֵן - *with grace*
2. וּלְחֶסֶד - *and with kindness*
3. וּלְרַחֲמִים - *and with mercy*
4. וּלְרֶוַח - *and for relief [from our troubles]*
5. הַצָּלָה - *by saving [us]*
6. וְהַצְלָחָה - *and success*
7. בְּרָכָה - *blessing*
8. וִישׁוּעָה - *and help*
9. נֶחָמָה - *comfort*
10. פַּרְנָסָה - *a way of making a living*
11. וְכַלְכָּלָה - *taking care of our needs*
12. וְרַחֲמִים - *and mercy*
13. וְחַיִּים - *and life*
14. וְשָׁלוֹם - *and peace*
15. וְכָל טוֹב - *and all good*

In times past, a man would normally eat fifteen meals a week. Each weekday he would eat one meal in the morning and one in the afternoon. These twelve meals, plus three meals on Shabbos, equal a total of fifteen meals. The fifteen blessings above stand for the fifteen meals which Hashem gives us each week. (*Iyun Tefillah*)

"וּמִכָּל טוּב לְעוֹלָם אַל יְחַסְּרֵנוּ" - *and Hashem should never let us lack anything good.*

Even if a person lives in a desert, Hashem will send him food. We see this by *Eliyahu Hanavi*, Elijah the Prophet. When he was forced to go into hiding, Hashem sent ravens to bring him food. (*Rabbeinu Bachya, Shaar Haparnassah*)

52

May the Merciful One, rule over us forever.

This group of *Harachamans* was written by our great Rabbis for the guest to bless his host. Since we are going to make a *beracha* on wine at the end of *Birkas Hamazon*, we might think that these *Harachamans* are an interruption between the last *beracha* of *bentching*

and the *kos shel beracha*. However, since it was included in *bentching* for the guest to bless his host, it is not considered an interruption. (*Avudraham*) "A person should first praise Hashem and then pray for the things he needs." (*Berachos* 32B) Therefore, the first three *Harachamans* are praises of Hashem.

May the Merciful One be blessed in heaven and on earth.

"What Power is there in heaven or earth who can do the great things that You do." (*Devarim* 3:24) You are not like a human king who has advisers who can stop him when he wants to do an act of kindness. Only You, Hashem, can change a bad decree, even if the person does not deserve Your kindness. (*Rashi*) We are to desire Eretz Yisrael. If Eretz Yisrael is desirable to us, we should watch the mitzvos of Hashem, so we will not be exiled from the land. (*Even Ezra*)

Hashem Will Be Praised, Glorified and is Great

May the Merciful One be praised in every generation, and through us may Hashem be glorified forever and ever and be honored through us forever, until the end of time.

From grandfather to father to grandson - each generation will add to the praises of the previous generation. The appreciation for the wonders of Hashem will increase, as each grandson adds to the praises his grandfather never saw. His grandfather did the same when he was a boy, praising Hashem for the additional things he sees that the previous generation did not.

Tiferes is the greatness of Hashem, that can be seen when a person behaves properly. When we pray properly after eating this is called *hadar* (adornment), Hashem sends down a flow of blessing to the world. This makes the world run smoothly. When we do the *mitzvos* in the best possible way, we cause people to realize Hashem's greatness. Saying the *Birkas Hamazon* properly with happiness and concentration and appreciation is one of the ultimate ways of adorning the name of Hashem.

הָרַחֲמָן הוּא יְפַרְנְסֵנוּ בְּכָבוֹד.
הָרַחֲמָן הוּא יִשְׁבּוֹר עֻלֵּנוּ מֵעַל צַוָּארֵנוּ, וְהוּא יוֹלִיכֵנוּ קוֹמְמִיּוּת לְאַרְצֵנוּ.

Hashem Supports Us With Honor and Guides Us to Our Land

May the Merciful One support us with honor. May the Merciful One break the yoke of oppression from our necks and He will deliver us with dignity and pride to our land.

"But also I will bring judgment against the nation who makes them slaves; and they will then leave with great wealth." (*Bereishis* 15:14) This verse comes to teach us that Egypt will be destroyed for making the Jewish people slaves. By using the expression "but also," the Torah explains that the four kingdoms where we were exiled will be destroyed along with Egypt. These were: 1. Bavel (Babylonia) 2. Paras (Persia) 3. Yavan (Greece) 4. Edom (Rome). [*Rashi, Sofseh Chahomim*]

The *Gur Aryeh* adds that Hashem has the power to take care of our needs without any effort at all on our part.

56

הָרַחֲמָן הוּא יִשְׁלַח לָנוּ בְּרָכָה מְרֻבָּה בַּבַּיִת הַזֶּה, וְעַל שֻׁלְחָן זֶה
שֶׁאָכַלְנוּ עָלָיו.

Send Us Blessing

May the Merciful One send great blessing to this house, and on this table where we have eaten.

"When three people eat together at one table and speak words of Torah, it is as if they have eaten from Hashem's table." (*Pirkei Avos* 3:4) "A Jew has the ability to make a table." (*Pirkei Avos* 3:4) A Jew has the ability to make even his simplest actions count as *mitzvos*. How? If he has in mind that he is eating so that he will have the strength to serve Hashem, then his eating is a *mitzvah*. (*Tiferes Yisroel*)

57

הָרַחֲמָן הוּא יִשְׁלַח לָנוּ אֶת אֵלִיָּהוּ הַנָּבִיא זָכוּר לַטּוֹב, וִיבַשֶּׂר לָנוּ בְּשׂוֹרוֹת טוֹבוֹת יְשׁוּעוֹת וְנֶחָמוֹת.

Send Elijah to Announce the Coming of Moshiach

May the Merciful One send us Elijah the Prophet, remembered for good, and may He bring us good news of saving us and comforting us.

Just as Elijah was sent to save us so many times in the past, so will he be sent in the future to announce the coming of *Moshiach*. (*Iyun Tefillah*)

Guests Say a Special Blessing for Their Host

The Guest's Blessing - Guests add this blessing for their host (Tur Orach Chayim 201):

"May it be Hashem's will that the host should not be embarrassed or ashamed in this World or the World to Come. May he be successful with all that he owns, and may all that he owns grow and multiply and be close to the city. May the Satan have no power over anything he does, and may no sin or thoughts of sin go through his mind, now or ever."

59

Guests say:

הָרַחֲמָן הוּא יְבָרֵךְ אֶת בַּעַל הַבַּיִת הַזֶּה, וְאֶת אִשְׁתּוֹ בַּעֲלַת הַבַּיִת הַזֶּה,
אוֹתָם וְאֶת בֵּיתָם וְאֶת זַרְעָם וְאֶת כָּל אֲשֶׁר לָהֶם.

Children eating at their parents' table say this blessing:

הָרַחֲמָן הוּא יְבָרֵךְ אֶת אָבִי מוֹרִי בַּעַל הַבַּיִת הַזֶּה, וְאֶת אִמִּי מוֹרָתִי
בַּעֲלַת הַבַּיִת הַזֶּה, אוֹתָם וְאֶת בֵּיתָם וְאֶת זַרְעָם וְאֶת כָּל אֲשֶׁר לָהֶם.

Those eating at their own table say:

הָרַחֲמָן הוּא יְבָרֵךְ אוֹתִי (וְאֶת אִשְׁתִּי/וְאֶת בַּעֲלִי. וְאֶת זַרְעִי) וְאֶת כָּל
אֲשֶׁר לִי.

The host blesses those who are joining him at his table:

וְאֶת כָּל הַמְסוּבִּין כָּאן.

Blessings to Add When They Apply

Guests add these blessings. Children eating at their parents' table should add the words in parentheses.

May the Merciful One bless (my father, my teacher) the man of this house, and (my mother, my teacher) the woman of this house, them, and their home, and their children, and everything that is theirs.

When eating at your own table, add the words that apply.

May the Merciful One bless me, (my wife/my husband, and my children) and all that is mine.

This blessing may be added when it applies.

And all that are sitting here.

אוֹתָנוּ וְאֶת כָּל אֲשֶׁר לָנוּ, כְּמוֹ שֶׁנִּתְבָּרְכוּ אֲבוֹתֵינוּ אַבְרָהָם יִצְחָק וְיַעֲקֹב
בַּכֹּל מִכֹּל כֹּל, כֵּן יְבָרֵךְ אוֹתָנוּ כֻּלָּנוּ יַחַד בִּבְרָכָה שְׁלֵמָה, וְנֹאמַר, אָמֵן.

The Blessing of Our Forefathers

שְׁלוֹשֶׁת
אֲבוֹת הַקְּדוֹשִׁים:

אברהם
("בכל")

יצחק ("מכל")

יעקב
("כל")

And each of us and all that belongs to us just as our forefathers Abraham, Isaac, and Jacob were blessed, with all, from all, and in every way. So may He bless us together with a complete blessing. May this be His will, and let us say Amen.

In *Baba Basra* 17a, they discuss the blessing of *bakol, mikol kol* - with all, from all, and in every way. These words come to teach us that Hashem gave our forefathers Avraham, Isaac, and Jacob a chance to taste a little bit of the World to Come while still in this world. They enjoyed this special blessing in many parts of their lives, and did not lack anything. (*Rashi*)

Each *kol* stands for a different blessing:

1. בכל - with all - "Hashem blessed Avraham with all things." (*Bereishis* 24:1) *Ibn Ezra* explains that "with all" includes long life, wealth, children, and those things which are valuable to a person.

2. מכל - from all - "I (Yitzchak) have eaten from all of it before you came." (*Bereishis* 27:33) Rashi explains that the food which Yaakov brought Yitzchak was so wonderous that it tasted like whatever Yitzchak wanted.

13. כל - and in every way - When Yaakov meets Eisav, he asks him to accept his present. "For Hashem has favored me and I have everything." (*Bereishis* 33:11) *Rashi* teaches us the difference in the way these two brothers spoke. Eisav talked like a big shot, saying that he had much more than he needed. Yaakov, on the other hand, said that Hashem blessed him with all that he needs.

Hashem blessed our forefathers with a complete blessing. It was perfect and did not lack anything. Since they fought so hard against the *yetzer hara*, Hashem protected them from the *yetzer hara* in their lifetimes, and it had no power over them in their deaths. Their souls were taken by Hashem Himself. (*Maharsha*)

61

Peace and Harmony

In Heaven, may they and we be deserving that we should have the protection of peace.

"A dry piece of bread in peace is better than a house full of feasting, with fighting." (*Mishlei* 17:1) It is better for man to eat a plain slice of dry bread in peace, than to eat a big piece of meat in a place where there is fighting. (*Ralbag*)

a

וְנִשָּׂא בְרָכָה מֵאֵת ה', וּצְדָקָה מֵאֱלֹקֵי יִשְׁעֵנוּ, וְנִמְצָא חֵן וְשֵׂכֶל טוֹב בְּעֵינֵי אֱלֹקִים וְאָדָם.

A Prayer to Find Favor

And may we get a blessing from Hashem, and kindness from the G-d who saves us. And let us find favor and understanding in the eyes of G-d and man.

"And you should find favor and understanding in the eyes of G-d and man." (*Mishlei* 3:4) If a person keeps the laws of the Torah, he will find favor in the eyes of Hashem and man. (*Ralbag*) Such a person will find favor and get a deeper understanding of life. (*Metzudas David*)

63

On *Shabbos* add:

הָרַחֲמָן הוּא יַנְחִילֵנוּ יוֹם שֶׁכֻּלוֹ שַׁבָּת וּמְנוּחָה לְחַיֵּי הָעוֹלָמִים.

On *Rosh Chodesh* add:

הָרַחֲמָן הוּא יְחַדֵּשׁ עָלֵינוּ אֶת הַחֹדֶשׁ הַזֶּה לְטוֹבָה וְלִבְרָכָה.

On *Festivals* add:

הָרַחֲמָן הוּא יַנְחִילֵנוּ יוֹם שֶׁכֻּלוֹ טוֹב.

On *Rosh Hashanah* add:

הָרַחֲמָן הוּא יְחַדֵּשׁ עָלֵינוּ אֶת הַשָּׁנָה הַזֹּאת לְטוֹבָה וְלִבְרָכָה.

On *Sukkos* add:

הָרַחֲמָן הוּא יָקִים לָנוּ אֶת סֻכַּת דָּוִד הַנּוֹפֶלֶת.

On *Chanukah* or *Purim* when *Al Hanissim* was forgotten, add:

הָרַחֲמָן הוּא יַעֲשֶׂה לָנוּ נִסִּים וְנִפְלָאוֹת כַּאֲשֶׁר עָשָׂה לַאֲבוֹתֵינוּ בַּיָּמִים הָהֵם בַּזְּמַן הַזֶּה.

Continue with: ...בִּימֵי מָרְדְּכַי or ...בִּימֵי מַתִּתְיָהוּ

For Special Occasions

ON SHABBOS:
"May the Merciful One bring us a world that will be all Shabbos and rest in the World to Come for eternal life."

ON ROSH CHODESH (the new month):
"May the Merciful One bring us this new month for good and for blessing."

ON FESTIVALS:
"May the Merciful One bring us the day which is completely good."

ON THE NEW YEAR:
"May the Merciful One bring us this new year for good and for blessing."

ON SUKKOS:
"May the Merciful One raise up for us the sukkah of King David which has fallen."

If a person forgot to say Al Hanissim for Purim or Chanukah, which is usually said after the blessing of nodeh, he should begin here by saying:

"May the Merciful One do miracles and wonders for us, just like He did for our forefathers in those days at this time."

Then, he should continue with *Bimei*.

64

הָרַחֲמָן הוּא יְזַכֵּנוּ לִימוֹת הַמָּשִׁיחַ וּלְחַיֵּי הָעוֹלָם הַבָּא.

Bring Us Moshiach

May the Merciful One let us be deserving of the days of Moshiach and the life of the World to Come.

"I will bless her with plenty of food, I will satisfy her poor with bread." (*Tehillim* 132:15) The crops in *Eretz Yisrael* will be blessed and even the poor will be able to fill up with bread. "There I will bring out the light of King David, I have prepared a lamp for My *Moshiach*." (*Tehillim* 132:17) Hashem will give power to *Moshiach*, and has prepared the Torah for *Moshiach* to use as a light. Jerusalem will become the center of blessings. From Jerusalem (Zion) will come the blessing that the poor will have enough food and that *Moshiach* will come to power. (*Metsudas David*)

מַגְדִּיל יְשׁוּעוֹת מַלְכּוֹ

On the Shabbos, Festivals, Chol Hamoed,
and Rosh Chodesh

מִגְדּוֹל יְשׁוּעוֹת מַלְכּוֹ

וְעֹשֶׂה חֶסֶד לִמְשִׁיחוֹ לְדָוִד וּלְזַרְעוֹ עַד עוֹלָם.

Magdil or *Migdol* - When?

בשבת:

מִגְדּוֹל

בחול:

מַגְדִּיל

ON WEEKDAYS ONLY:
"מגדיל ישועות מלכו" - *He makes great victories for His king*

SHABBOS, FESTIVALS, CHOL HAMOED, and ROSH CHODESH, SAY:
"מגדול ישועות מלכו" - *He is a tower of strength to His king*

ALL CONTINUE:
"ועשה חסד למשיחו לדוד ולזרעו עד עולם." - *and does kindness to His Moshiach, to David and his children forever. [Tehillim 18:51] [Samuel II 22:51]*

Magdil is a verb. We use a verb on weekdays, since a verb tells us that something is happening. Exile is compared to the weekdays. Hashem is doing things. Each day, He is busy preparing for the final *Beis Hamikdash* and getting ready to take us out of exile. *Magdil*, the verb, comes to show us that each day is getting closer to the time of *Moshiach* and the end of our exile.

Migdol is a noun, used in the Shabbos and Yom Tov *bentching*, which stands for something whole or complete. Both Shabbos and Yom Tov are compared to the days of *Moshiach*. All three are a completion. Shabbos is a completion of the days of the week. The days of *Moshiach* are a completion of the long exile. At this time, we say, "Hashem is a tower." He is like a strong, safe place. (*Iyun Tefillah*)

עֹשֶׂה שָׁלוֹם בִּמְרוֹמָיו, הוּא יַעֲשֶׂה שָׁלוֹם עָלֵינוּ וְעַל כָּל יִשְׂרָאֵל. וְאִמְרוּ, אָמֵן.

A Prayer for Peace

He who makes peace in His heavens, may He make peace for us and for all Israel, and say, Amen.

"Rule and fear are with Him, He makes peace in His high places." (*Iyov* 25:2) Hashem's kingdom is great. He makes peace in the heavens, so each angel does exactly what Hashem wants him to do. They do not fight with each other, but instead, work peacefully with one another. They know that Hashem has unlimited power to punish anyone who does not do His will. If angels, who do not have man's weaknesses and faults, understand and fear Hashem, how much more so should human beings, who get into fights easily, be aware of Hashem's power. (*Metzudas David, Etz Yosef*)

67

יְראוּ אֶת ה' קְדֹשָׁיו, כִּי אֵין מַחְסוֹר לִירֵאָיו.

Fear Only Hashem

Let His holy people fear G-d, because those who fear Him will not lack anything. (Tehillim 34:10)

We are Hashem's chosen people. We should fear only Him and nothing else. Other nations worship their idols which are useless. They are afraid of punishment. Their religious leaders separate themselves from normal life. They think that to be holy means not to have any joy in this world. However, that is not what Hashem wants. He wants us to use the pleasures of this world according to the rules of the Torah. This is the way to serve Hashem. (*Malbim*)

68

כְּפִירִים רָשׁוּ וְרָעֵבוּ, וְדֹרְשֵׁי ה׳ לֹא יַחְסְרוּ כָל טוֹב.

Hashem Will Always Make Sure That We Have Food

Young lions may suffer hunger, but those who look to Hashem will not lack any good thing. [Tehillim 34:11]

Hashem provides food for all creatures, from the tiniest to the strongest of animals. It does not matter how strong an animal is. Even the mightiest lion which is a terrific hunter can go hungry. We depend on Hashem, alone, to give us our food. When a lion is no longer able to hunt, he may starve. But the person who does Hashem's will does not have to worry. Even when he becomes old and weak, he will have food. Hashem has already prepared it for him. (*Malbim*)

69

הוֹדוּ לַה' כִּי טוֹב, כִּי לְעוֹלָם חַסְדּוֹ. פּוֹתֵחַ אֶת יָדֶךָ, וּמַשְׂבִּיעַ לְכָל חַי רָצוֹן.

Give Thanks to Hashem

Give thanks to Hashem because He is good; His kindess is forever. (Tehillim 118:1) You open Your hand and provide the needs of all living things. (Tehillim 145:16)

"הוֹדוּ לַה' כִּי טוֹב כִּי לְעוֹלָם חַסְדּוֹ" - *Give thanks to Hashem because He is good; His kindness is forever. [Tehillim 118:1]*

Every nation of the world will give thanks to Hashem for His goodness and His kindness. (*Malbim*)

"פּוֹתֵחַ אֶת יָדֶךָ וּמַשְׂבִּיעַ לְכָל חַי רָצוֹן" - *You open Your hand and provide the needs of all living things. [Tehillim 145:16]*

Hashem blesses us with plenty, according to His will. He gives us much more than we need to live. (*Iyun Tefillah*)

70

בָּרוּךְ הַגֶּבֶר אֲשֶׁר יִבְטַח בַּה׳ וְהָיָה ה׳ מִבְטַחוֹ.

Trust in Hashem

Blessed is the man who trusts in Hashem, and Hashem will be his trust. [Yirmiyahu 17:7]

The more a person trusts in Hashem, the more Hashem helps him. (*Metsudas David*)

71

נַעַר הָיִיתִי גַּם זָקַנְתִּי, וְלֹא רָאִיתִי צַדִּיק נֶעֱזָב, וְזַרְעוֹ מְבַקֶּשׁ לָחֶם.

Hashem Will Always Be With Us

I was young and now I am old, and I have never seen Hashem forget about a righteous man, or his children having to beg for bread. [Tehillim 37:25]

If the righteous man is not successful, his children will be successful. Because of the good deeds of this righteous father, Hashem will have mercy and bless his children. (*Malbim*)

Hashem will give His people strength, Hashem will bless His nation with peace. [Tehillim 29:11]

The days of *Moshiach* will soon be here. When he comes, those who serve Hashem will get stronger and Hashem will bless His nation with peace. There will no longer be wars. (*Metzudas David*)

73

סדר
ברכת המזון

Mayim Acharonim

After eating a meal with bread, a person must wash one's hands before saying the *Birkas Hamazon*. This washing of hands is called *mayim acharonim*. One may not talk for any reason after washing one's hands until after the *Birkas Hamazon*. Even words of *Torah* are forbidden.

BIRKAS HAMAZON

Psalm 137 is said before *Birkas Hamazon* on weekdays. It speaks about the destruction of the *Beis Hamikdash*.

עַל נַהֲרוֹת בָּבֶל, שָׁם יָשַׁבְנוּ גַּם בָּכִינוּ, בְּזָכְרֵנוּ אֶת צִיּוֹן. עַל עֲרָבִים בְּתוֹכָהּ תָּלִינוּ כִּנּרוֹתֵינוּ. כִּי שָׁם שְׁאֵלוּנוּ שׁוֹבֵינוּ דִּבְרֵי שִׁיר וְתוֹלָלֵינוּ שִׂמְחָה, שִׁירוּ לָנוּ מִשִּׁיר צִיּוֹן. אֵיךְ נָשִׁיר אֶת שִׁיר ה', עַל אַדְמַת נֵכָר. אִם אֶשְׁכָּחֵךְ יְרוּשָׁלָיִם, תִּשְׁכַּח יְמִינִי. תִּדְבַּק לְשׁוֹנִי לְחִכִּי, אִם לֹא אֶזְכְּרֵכִי, אִם לֹא אַעֲלֶה אֶת יְרוּשָׁלַיִם עַל רֹאשׁ שִׂמְחָתִי. זְכֹר ה' לִבְנֵי אֱדוֹם אֵת יוֹם יְרוּשָׁלָיִם, הָאֹמְרִים עָרוּ עָרוּ, עַד הַיְסוֹד בָּהּ. בַּת בָּבֶל הַשְּׁדוּדָה אַשְׁרֵי שֶׁיְשַׁלֶּם לָךְ אֶת גְּמוּלֵךְ שֶׁגָּמַלְתְּ לָנוּ. אַשְׁרֵי שֶׁיֹּאחֵז וְנִפֵּץ אֶת עֹלָלַיִךְ אֶל הַסָּלַע.

Psalm 126 is said on *Shabbos*, *Yom Tov*, and at meals on other festive occasions such as weddings, circumcisions, or a *pidyon haben*.

שִׁיר הַמַּעֲלוֹת, בְּשׁוּב ה' אֶת שִׁיבַת צִיּוֹן, הָיִינוּ כְּחֹלְמִים. אָז יִמָּלֵא שְׂחוֹק פִּינוּ וּלְשׁוֹנֵנוּ רִנָּה, אָז יֹאמְרוּ בַגּוֹיִם, הִגְדִּיל ה' לַעֲשׂוֹת עִם אֵלֶּה. הִגְדִּיל ה' לַעֲשׂוֹת עִמָּנוּ, הָיִינוּ שְׂמֵחִים. שׁוּבָה ה' אֶת שְׁבִיתֵנוּ, כַּאֲפִיקִים בַּנֶּגֶב. הַזֹּרְעִים בְּדִמְעָה, בְּרִנָּה יִקְצֹרוּ. הָלוֹךְ יֵלֵךְ וּבָכֹה נֹשֵׂא מֶשֶׁךְ הַזָּרַע, בֹּא יָבֹא בְרִנָּה, נֹשֵׂא אֲלֻמֹּתָיו.

Before beginning the *Birkas Hamazon*, there is a custom to say the following:

לְשֵׁם יְחוּד קוּדְשָׁא בְּרִיךְ הוּא וּשְׁכִינְתֵּיהּ בִּדְחִילוּ וּרְחִימוּ לְיַחֵד שֵׁם י-ה בו-ח עַל יְדֵי הַהוּא טָמִיר וְנֶעְלָם בְּיִחוּדָא שְׁלִים בְּשֵׁם כָּל יִשְׂרָאֵל. הֲרֵינִי מוּכָן וּמְזוּמָּן לְקַיֵּים מִצְוַת עֲשֵׂה שֶׁל בִּרְכַּת הַמָּזוֹן שֶׁנֶּאֱמַר וְאָכַלְתָּ וְשָׂבָעְתָּ וּבֵרַכְתָּ אֶת ה' אֱלֹקֶיךָ עַל הָאָרֶץ הַטּוֹבָה אֲשֶׁר נָתַן לָךְ: וִיהִי נֹעַם ה' אֱלֹקֵינוּ עָלֵינוּ וּמַעֲשֵׂה יָדֵינוּ כּוֹנְנָה עָלֵינוּ וּמַעֲשֵׂה יָדֵינוּ כּוֹנְנֵהוּ:

If three or more men eat a meal together, one leads them in *Birkas Hamazon.*

Leader: רַבּוֹתַי נְבָרֵךְ.

Others : יְהִי שֵׁם ה' מְבֹרָךְ מֵעַתָּה וְעַד עוֹלָם.

If ten men eat a meal together, they add the words in parentheses.

Leader: יְהִי שֵׁם ה' מְבֹרָךְ מֵעַתָּה וְעַד עוֹלָם.
בִּרְשׁוּת מָרָנָן וְרַבָּנָן וְרַבּוֹתַי, נְבָרֵךְ (אֱלֹקֵינוּ)שֶׁאָכַלְנוּ מִשֶּׁלוֹ.

Others: בָּרוּךְ (אֱלֹקֵינוּ) שֶׁאָכַלְנוּ מִשֶּׁלוֹ וּבְטוּבוֹ חָיִינוּ.

Leader: בָּרוּךְ (אֱלֹקֵינוּ) שֶׁאָכַלְנוּ מִשֶּׁלוֹ וּבְטוּבוֹ חָיִינוּ.

If there are ten men, the leader continues and adds these words:
בָּרוּךְ הוּא וּבָרוּךְ שְׁמוֹ

בָּרוּךְ אַתָּה ה' אֱלֹקֵינוּ מֶלֶךְ הָעוֹלָם הַזָּן אֶת הָעוֹלָם כֻּלּוֹ, בְּטוּבוֹ, בְּחֵן בְּחֶסֶד וּבְרַחֲמִים, הוּא נוֹתֵן לֶחֶם לְכָל בָּשָׂר, כִּי לְעוֹלָם חַסְדּוֹ. וּבְטוּבוֹ הַגָּדוֹל, תָּמִיד לֹא חָסַר לָנוּ, וְאַל יֶחְסַר לָנוּ מָזוֹן לְעוֹלָם וָעֶד. בַּעֲבוּר שְׁמוֹ הַגָּדוֹל, כִּי הוּא אֵ-ל זָן וּמְפַרְנֵס לַכֹּל, וּמֵטִיב לַכֹּל, וּמֵכִין מָזוֹן לְכָל בְּרִיּוֹתָיו אֲשֶׁר בָּרָא. בָּרוּךְ אַתָּה ה', הַזָּן אֶת הַכֹּל.

נוֹדֶה לְךָ ה' אֱלֹקֵינוּ, עַל שֶׁהִנְחַלְתָּ לַאֲבוֹתֵינוּ אֶרֶץ חֶמְדָּה טוֹבָה וּרְחָבָה. וְעַל שֶׁהוֹצֵאתָנוּ ה' אֱלֹקֵינוּ מֵאֶרֶץ מִצְרַיִם, וּפְדִיתָנוּ מִבֵּית עֲבָדִים, וְעַל בְּרִיתְךָ שֶׁחָתַמְתָּ בִּבְשָׂרֵנוּ, וְעַל תּוֹרָתְךָ שֶׁלִּמַּדְתָּנוּ, וְעַל חֻקֶּיךָ שֶׁהוֹדַעְתָּנוּ, וְעַל חַיִּים חֵן וָחֶסֶד שֶׁחוֹנַנְתָּנוּ, וְעַל אֲכִילַת מָזוֹן שֶׁאַתָּה זָן וּמְפַרְנֵס אוֹתָנוּ תָּמִיד, בְּכָל יוֹם וּבְכָל עֵת וּבְכָל שָׁעָה.

On *Chanukah* add:

וְעַל הַנִּסִּים וְעַל הַפֻּרְקָן וְעַל הַגְּבוּרוֹת וְעַל הַתְּשׁוּעוֹת וְעַל הַמִּלְחָמוֹת שֶׁעָשִׂיתָ
לַאֲבוֹתֵינוּ בַּיָּמִים הָהֵם בַּזְּמַן הַזֶּה:

בִּימֵי מַתִּתְיָהוּ בֶּן יוֹחָנָן כֹּהֵן גָּדוֹל חַשְׁמוֹנָאִי וּבָנָיו, כְּשֶׁעָמְדָה מַלְכוּת יָוָן
הָרְשָׁעָה עַל עַמְּךָ יִשְׂרָאֵל, לְהַשְׁכִּיחָם תּוֹרָתֶךָ, וּלְהַעֲבִירָם מֵחֻקֵּי רְצוֹנֶךָ. וְאַתָּה
בְּרַחֲמֶיךָ הָרַבִּים, עָמַדְתָּ לָהֶם בְּעֵת צָרָתָם, רַבְתָּ אֶת רִיבָם, דַּנְתָּ אֶת דִּינָם, נָקַמְתָּ
אֶת נִקְמָתָם. מָסַרְתָּ גִבּוֹרִים בְּיַד חַלָּשִׁים, וְרַבִּים בְּיַד מְעַטִּים, וּטְמֵאִים בְּיַד
טְהוֹרִים, וּרְשָׁעִים בְּיַד צַדִּיקִים, וְזֵדִים בְּיַד עוֹסְקֵי תוֹרָתֶךָ. וּלְךָ עָשִׂיתָ שֵׁם גָּדוֹל
וְקָדוֹשׁ בְּעוֹלָמֶךָ, וּלְעַמְּךָ יִשְׂרָאֵל עָשִׂיתָ תְּשׁוּעָה גְדוֹלָה וּפֻרְקָן כְּהַיּוֹם הַזֶּה. וְאַחַר
כֵּן בָּאוּ בָנֶיךָ לִדְבִיר בֵּיתֶךָ, וּפִנּוּ אֶת הֵיכָלֶךָ, וְטִהֲרוּ אֶת מִקְדָּשֶׁךָ, וְהִדְלִיקוּ נֵרוֹת
בְּחַצְרוֹת קָדְשֶׁךָ, וְקָבְעוּ שְׁמוֹנַת יְמֵי חֲנֻכָּה אֵלּוּ, לְהוֹדוֹת וּלְהַלֵּל לְשִׁמְךָ הַגָּדוֹל.

Prayer of thanks for the miracles of *Purim:*

וְעַל הַנִּסִּים וְעַל הַפֻּרְקָן וְעַל הַגְּבוּרוֹת וְעַל הַתְּשׁוּעוֹת וְעַל הַמִּלְחָמוֹת שֶׁעָשִׂיתָ
לַאֲבוֹתֵינוּ בַּיָּמִים הָהֵם בַּזְּמַן הַזֶּה:

בִּימֵי מָרְדְּכַי וְאֶסְתֵּר בְּשׁוּשַׁן הַבִּירָה, כְּשֶׁעָמַד עֲלֵיהֶם הָמָן הָרָשָׁע, בִּקֵּשׁ לְהַשְׁמִיד
לַהֲרֹג וּלְאַבֵּד אֶת כָּל הַיְּהוּדִים, מִנַּעַר וְעַד זָקֵן, טַף וְנָשִׁים בְּיוֹם אֶחָד, בִּשְׁלוֹשָׁה
עָשָׂר לְחֹדֶשׁ שְׁנֵים עָשָׂר, הוּא חֹדֶשׁ אֲדָר, וּשְׁלָלָם לָבוֹז. וְאַתָּה בְּרַחֲמֶיךָ הָרַבִּים
הֵפַרְתָּ אֶת עֲצָתוֹ, וְקִלְקַלְתָּ אֶת מַחֲשַׁבְתּוֹ, וַהֲשֵׁבוֹתָ לּוֹ גְּמוּלוֹ בְּרֹאשׁוֹ, וְתָלוּ אוֹתוֹ
וְאֶת בָּנָיו עַל הָעֵץ.

וְעַל הַכֹּל ה׳ אֱלֹקֵינוּ אֲנַחְנוּ מוֹדִים לָךְ, וּמְבָרְכִים אוֹתָךְ, יִתְבָּרַךְ שִׁמְךָ בְּפִי כָּל חַי
תָּמִיד לְעוֹלָם וָעֶד. כַּכָּתוּב, וְאָכַלְתָּ וְשָׂבָעְתָּ, וּבֵרַכְתָּ אֶת ה׳ אֱלֹקֵיךָ, עַל הָאָרֶץ
הַטֹּבָה אֲשֶׁר נָתַן לָךְ. בָּרוּךְ אַתָּה ה׳, עַל הָאָרֶץ וְעַל הַמָּזוֹן.

רַחֵם ה׳ אֱלֹקֵינוּ עַל יִשְׂרָאֵל עַמֶּךָ, וְעַל יְרוּשָׁלַיִם עִירֶךָ, וְעַל צִיּוֹן מִשְׁכַּן כְּבוֹדֶךָ,
וְעַל מַלְכוּת בֵּית דָּוִד מְשִׁיחֶךָ, וְעַל הַבַּיִת הַגָּדוֹל וְהַקָּדוֹשׁ שֶׁנִּקְרָא שִׁמְךָ עָלָיו.
אֱלֹקֵינוּ אָבִינוּ רְעֵנוּ זוּנֵנוּ פַּרְנְסֵנוּ וְכַלְכְּלֵנוּ וְהַרְוִיחֵנוּ, וְהַרְוַח לָנוּ ה׳ אֱלֹקֵינוּ מְהֵרָה
מִכָּל צָרוֹתֵינוּ. וְנָא אַל תַּצְרִיכֵנוּ ה׳ אֱלֹקֵינוּ, לֹא לִידֵי מַתְּנַת בָּשָׂר וָדָם, וְלֹא לִידֵי
הַלְוָאָתָם, כִּי אִם לְיָדְךָ הַמְּלֵאָה הַפְּתוּחָה הַקְּדוֹשָׁה וְהָרְחָבָה, שֶׁלֹּא נֵבוֹשׁ וְלֹא
נִכָּלֵם לְעוֹלָם וָעֶד.

Shabbos prayer:

רְצֵה וְהַחֲלִיצֵנוּ ה' אֱלֹקֵינוּ בְּמִצְוֹתֶיךָ, וּבְמִצְוַת יוֹם הַשְּׁבִיעִי הַשַּׁבָּת הַגָּדוֹל
וְהַקָּדוֹשׁ הַזֶּה, כִּי יוֹם זֶה גָּדוֹל וְקָדוֹשׁ הוּא לְפָנֶיךָ, לִשְׁבָּת בּוֹ וְלָנוּחַ בּוֹ בְּאַהֲבָה
כְּמִצְוַת רְצוֹנֶךָ, וּבִרְצוֹנְךָ הָנִיחַ לָנוּ ה' אֱלֹקֵינוּ, שֶׁלֹּא תְהֵא צָרָה וְיָגוֹן וַאֲנָחָה בְּיוֹם
מְנוּחָתֵנוּ, וְהַרְאֵנוּ ה' אֱלֹקֵינוּ בְּנֶחָמַת צִיּוֹן עִירֶךָ, וּבְבִנְיַן יְרוּשָׁלַיִם עִיר קָדְשֶׁךָ, כִּי
אַתָּה הוּא בַּעַל הַיְשׁוּעוֹת וּבַעַל הַנֶּחָמוֹת.

Prayer added on the New Moon, New Year, and Festivals:

אֱלֹקֵינוּ וֵאלֹקֵי אֲבוֹתֵינוּ, יַעֲלֶה, וְיָבֹא, וְיַגִּיעַ, וְיֵרָאֶה, וְיֵרָצֶה, וְיִשָּׁמַע, וְיִפָּקֵד, וְיִזָּכֵר
זִכְרוֹנֵנוּ וּפִקְדוֹנֵנוּ, וְזִכְרוֹן אֲבוֹתֵינוּ, וְזִכְרוֹן מָשִׁיחַ בֶּן דָּוִד עַבְדֶּךָ, וְזִכְרוֹן יְרוּשָׁלַיִם
עִיר קָדְשֶׁךָ, וְזִכְרוֹן כָּל עַמְּךָ בֵּית יִשְׂרָאֵל לְפָנֶיךָ, לִפְלֵיטָה לְטוֹבָה לְחֵן וּלְחֶסֶד
וּלְרַחֲמִים, לְחַיִּים וּלְשָׁלוֹם בְּיוֹם:

Rosh Chodesh: רֹאשׁ הַחֹדֶשׁ הַזֶּה.
Passover: חַג הַמַּצּוֹת הַזֶּה.
Shavuos: חַג הַשָּׁבֻעוֹת הַזֶּה.
Sukkos: חַג הַסֻּכּוֹת הַזֶּה.
Shemini Atzeres and Simchas Torah: הַשְּׁמִינִי חַג הָעֲצֶרֶת הַזֶּה.
Rosh Hashanah: הַזִּכָּרוֹן הַזֶּה.

זָכְרֵנוּ ה' אֱלֹקֵינוּ בּוֹ לְטוֹבָה, וּפָקְדֵנוּ בּוֹ לִבְרָכָה, וְהוֹשִׁיעֵנוּ בּוֹ לְחַיִּים. וּבִדְבַר
יְשׁוּעָה וְרַחֲמִים, חוּס וְחָנֵּנוּ וְרַחֵם עָלֵינוּ וְהוֹשִׁיעֵנוּ, כִּי אֵלֶיךָ עֵינֵינוּ, כִּי א-ל (On -
Rosh Hashanah add מֶלֶךְ) חַנּוּן וְרַחוּם אָתָּה.

וּבְנֵה יְרוּשָׁלַיִם עִיר הַקֹּדֶשׁ בִּמְהֵרָה בְיָמֵינוּ. בָּרוּךְ אַתָּה ה', בּוֹנֵה בְרַחֲמָיו
יְרוּשָׁלָיִם. אָמֵן.

בָּרוּךְ אַתָּה ה' אֱלֹקֵינוּ מֶלֶךְ הָעוֹלָם, הָא-ל אָבִינוּ מַלְכֵּנוּ אַדִּירֵנוּ בּוֹרְאֵנוּ גּוֹאֲלֵנוּ
יוֹצְרֵנוּ קְדוֹשֵׁנוּ קְדוֹשׁ יַעֲקֹב, רוֹעֵנוּ רוֹעֵה יִשְׂרָאֵל, הַמֶּלֶךְ הַטּוֹב וְהַמֵּטִיב לַכֹּל,
שֶׁבְּכָל יוֹם וָיוֹם הוּא הֵטִיב, הוּא מֵטִיב, הוּא יֵיטִיב לָנוּ. הוּא גְמָלָנוּ הוּא גוֹמְלֵנוּ
הוּא יִגְמְלֵנוּ לָעַד, לְחֵן וּלְחֶסֶד וּלְרַחֲמִים וּלְרֶוַח הַצָּלָה וְהַצְלָחָה, בְּרָכָה וִישׁוּעָה
נֶחָמָה פַּרְנָסָה וְכַלְכָּלָה וְרַחֲמִים וְחַיִּים וְשָׁלוֹם וְכָל טוֹב, וּמִכָּל טוּב לְעוֹלָם אַל
יְחַסְּרֵנוּ:

הָרַחֲמָן הוּא יִמְלוֹךְ עָלֵינוּ לְעוֹלָם וָעֶד.

הָרַחֲמָן הוּא יִתְבָּרַךְ בַּשָּׁמַיִם וּבָאָרֶץ.

הָרַחֲמָן הוּא יִשְׁתַּבַּח לְדוֹר דּוֹרִים, וְיִתְפָּאַר בָּנוּ לָעַד וּלְנֵצַח נְצָחִים, וְיִתְהַדַּר בָּנוּ לָעַד וּלְעוֹלְמֵי עוֹלָמִים.

הָרַחֲמָן הוּא יְפַרְנְסֵנוּ בְּכָבוֹד.

הָרַחֲמָן הוּא יִשְׁבּוֹר עֻלֵּנוּ מֵעַל צַוָּארֵנוּ, וְהוּא יוֹלִיכֵנוּ קוֹמְמִיּוּת לְאַרְצֵנוּ.

הָרַחֲמָן הוּא יִשְׁלַח לָנוּ בְּרָכָה מְרֻבָּה בַּבַּיִת הַזֶּה, וְעַל שֻׁלְחָן זֶה שֶׁאָכַלְנוּ עָלָיו.

הָרַחֲמָן הוּא יִשְׁלַח לָנוּ אֶת אֵלִיָּהוּ הַנָּבִיא זָכוּר לַטּוֹב, וִיבַשֶּׂר לָנוּ בְּשׂוֹרוֹת טוֹבוֹת יְשׁוּעוֹת וְנֶחָמוֹת.

Guests say a special blessing for their host:

יְהִי רָצוֹן שֶׁלֹּא יֵבוֹשׁ וְלֹא יִכָּלֵם בַּעַל הַבַּיִת הַזֶּה, לֹא בָעוֹלָם הַזֶּה וְלֹא בָעוֹלָם הַבָּא, וְיַצְלִיחַ בְּכָל נְכָסָיו, וְיִהְיוּ נְכָסָיו מוּצְלָחִים וּקְרוֹבִים לָעִיר, וְאַל יִשְׁלוֹט שָׂטָן בְּמַעֲשֵׂה יָדָיו, וְאַל יִזְדַּקֵּק לְפָנָיו שׁוּם דְּבַר חֵטְא וְהִרְהוּר עָוֹן, מֵעַתָּה וְעַד עוֹלָם.

Guests say:

הָרַחֲמָן הוּא יְבָרֵךְ אֶת בַּעַל הַבַּיִת הַזֶּה, וְאֶת אִשְׁתּוֹ בַּעֲלַת הַבַּיִת הַזֶּה, אוֹתָם וְאֶת בֵּיתָם וְאֶת זַרְעָם וְאֶת כָּל אֲשֶׁר לָהֶם.

Children eating at their parents' table say this blessing:

הָרַחֲמָן הוּא יְבָרֵךְ אֶת אָבִי מוֹרִי בַּעַל הַבַּיִת הַזֶּה, וְאֶת אִמִּי מוֹרָתִי בַּעֲלַת הַבַּיִת הַזֶּה, אוֹתָם וְאֶת בֵּיתָם וְאֶת זַרְעָם וְאֶת כָּל אֲשֶׁר לָהֶם.

Those eating at their own table say:

הָרַחֲמָן הוּא יְבָרֵךְ אוֹתִי (וְאֶת אִשְׁתִּי/וְאֶת בַּעֲלִי. וְאֶת זַרְעִי) וְאֶת כָּל אֲשֶׁר לִי.

The host blesses those who are joining him at his table:

וְאֶת כָּל הַמְסוּבִּין כָּאן.

Everyone continues:

אוֹתָנוּ וְאֶת כָּל אֲשֶׁר לָנוּ, כְּמוֹ שֶׁנִּתְבָּרְכוּ אֲבוֹתֵינוּ אַבְרָהָם יִצְחָק וְיַעֲקֹב בַּכֹּל מִכֹּל כֹּל, כֵּן יְבָרֵךְ אוֹתָנוּ כֻּלָּנוּ יַחַד בִּבְרָכָה שְׁלֵמָה, וְנֹאמַר, אָמֵן.

בַּמָּרוֹם יְלַמְּדוּ עֲלֵיהֶם וְעָלֵינוּ זְכוּת, שֶׁתְּהֵא לְמִשְׁמֶרֶת שָׁלוֹם. וְנִשָּׂא בְרָכָה מֵאֵת ה', וּצְדָקָה מֵאֱלֹקֵי יִשְׁעֵנוּ, וְנִמְצָא חֵן וְשֵׂכֶל טוֹב בְּעֵינֵי אֱלֹקִים וְאָדָם.

On *Shabbos* add:

הָרַחֲמָן הוּא יַנְחִילֵנוּ יוֹם שֶׁכֻּלּוֹ שַׁבָּת וּמְנוּחָה לְחַיֵּי הָעוֹלָמִים.

On *Rosh Chodesh* add:

הָרַחֲמָן הוּא יְחַדֵּשׁ עָלֵינוּ אֶת הַחֹדֶשׁ הַזֶּה לְטוֹבָה וְלִבְרָכָה.

On *Festivals* add:

הָרַחֲמָן הוּא יַנְחִילֵנוּ יוֹם שֶׁכֻּלּוֹ טוֹב.

On *Rosh Hashanah* add:

הָרַחֲמָן הוּא יְחַדֵּשׁ עָלֵינוּ אֶת הַשָּׁנָה הַזֹּאת לְטוֹבָה וְלִבְרָכָה.

On *Sukkos* add:

הָרַחֲמָן הוּא יָקִים לָנוּ אֶת סֻכַּת דָּוִיד הַנֹּפָלֶת.

On *Chanukah* or *Purim* when *Al Hanissim* was forgotten, add:

הָרַחֲמָן הוּא יַעֲשֶׂה לָנוּ נִסִּים וְנִפְלָאוֹת כַּאֲשֶׁר עָשָׂה לַאֲבוֹתֵינוּ בַּיָּמִים הָהֵם בַּזְּמַן הַזֶּה.

Continue with: ...בִּימֵי מָרְדְּכַי or ...בִּימֵי מַתִּתְיָהוּ

All continue here:

הָרַחֲמָן הוּא יְזַכֵּנוּ לִימוֹת הַמָּשִׁיחַ וּלְחַיֵּי הָעוֹלָם הַבָּא.

On weekdays:

מַגְדִּיל יְשׁוּעוֹת מַלְכּוֹ

On Shabbos, Yom Tov and Rosh Chodesh:

מִגְדּוֹל יְשׁוּעוֹת מַלְכּוֹ

וְעֹשֶׂה חֶסֶד לִמְשִׁיחוֹ לְדָוִד וּלְזַרְעוֹ עַד עוֹלָם. עֹשֶׂה שָׁלוֹם בִּמְרוֹמָיו, הוּא יַעֲשֶׂה שָׁלוֹם עָלֵינוּ וְעַל כָּל יִשְׂרָאֵל. וְאִמְרוּ, אָמֵן.

יְראוּ אֶת ה' קְדֹשָׁיו, כִּי אֵין מַחְסוֹר לִירֵאָיו. כְּפִירִים רָשׁוּ וְרָעֵבוּ, וְדֹרְשֵׁי ה' לֹא יַחְסְרוּ כָל טוֹב. הוֹדוּ לַה' כִּי טוֹב, כִּי לְעוֹלָם חַסְדּוֹ. פּוֹתֵחַ אֶת יָדֶךָ, וּמַשְׂבִּיעַ לְכָל חַי רָצוֹן. בָּרוּךְ הַגֶּבֶר אֲשֶׁר יִבְטַח בַּה', וְהָיָה ה' מִבְטַחוֹ. נַעַר הָיִיתִי גַּם זָקַנְתִּי, וְלֹא רָאִיתִי צַדִּיק נֶעֱזָב, וְזַרְעוֹ מְבַקֶּשׁ לָחֶם. ה' עֹז לְעַמּוֹ יִתֵּן, ה' יְבָרֵךְ אֶת עַמּוֹ בַשָּׁלוֹם.

BOREI NEFASHOS

בָּרוּךְ אַתָּה ח' אֱלֹקֵינוּ מֶלֶךְ הָעוֹלָם, בּוֹרֵא נְפָשׁוֹת רַבּוֹת וְחֶסְרוֹנָן, עַל כָּל מַה שֶׁבָּרָא(תָ) לְהַחֲיוֹת בָּהֶם נֶפֶשׁ כָּל חָי. בָּרוּךְ חֵי הָעוֹלָמִים.

BERACHA ACHARONAH

בָּרוּךְ אַתָּה ח' אֱלֹקֵינוּ מֶלֶךְ הָעוֹלָם,

After food products: עַל הַמִּחְיָה וְעַל הַכַּלְכָּלָה,

After Wine: עַל הַגֶּפֶן וְעַל פְּרִי הַגֶּפֶן,

After fruits עַל הָעֵץ וְעַל פְּרִי הָעֵץ,

וְעַל תְּנוּבַת הַשָּׂדֶה, וְעַל אֶרֶץ חֶמְדָּה טוֹבָה וּרְחָבָה, שֶׁרָצִיתָ וְהִנְחַלְתָּ לַאֲבוֹתֵינוּ, לֶאֱכוֹל מִפִּרְיָהּ וְלִשְׂבּוֹעַ מִטּוּבָהּ. רַחֵם ח' אֱלֹקֵינוּ עַל יִשְׂרָאֵל עַמֶּךָ, וְעַל יְרוּשָׁלַיִם עִירֶךָ, וְעַל צִיּוֹן מִשְׁכַּן כְּבוֹדֶךָ, וְעַל מִזְבְּחֶךָ וְעַל הֵיכָלֶךָ. וּבְנֵה יְרוּשָׁלַיִם עִיר הַקֹּדֶשׁ בִּמְהֵרָה בְיָמֵינוּ, וְהַעֲלֵנוּ לְתוֹכָהּ, וְשַׂמְּחֵנוּ בְּבִנְיָנָהּ, וְנֹאכַל מִפִּרְיָהּ, וְנִשְׂבַּע מִטּוּבָהּ, וּנְבָרֶכְךָ עָלֶיהָ בִּקְדֻשָּׁה וּבְטָהֳרָה.

On Shabbos: וּרְצֵה וְהַחֲלִיצֵנוּ בְּיוֹם הַשַּׁבָּת הַזֶּה.

On Rosh Chodesh: וְזָכְרֵנוּ לְטוֹבָה בְּיוֹם רֹאשׁ הַחֹדֶשׁ הַזֶּה.

On Pesach: וְשַׂמְּחֵנוּ בְּיוֹם חַג הַמַּצּוֹת הַזֶּה.

On Shavuos: וְשַׂמְּחֵנוּ בְּיוֹם חַג הַשָּׁבֻעוֹת הַזֶּה.

On Succos: וְשַׂמְּחֵנוּ בְּיוֹם חַג הַסֻּכּוֹת הַזֶּה.

On Shemini Atzeres/Simchas Torah:
וְשַׂמְּחֵנוּ בְּיוֹם הַשְּׁמִינִי חַג הָעֲצֶרֶת הַזֶּה.

On Rosh Hashanah:
וְזָכְרֵנוּ לְטוֹבָה בְּיוֹם הַזִּכָּרוֹן הַזֶּה.

כִּי אַתָּה ח' טוֹב וּמֵטִיב לַכֹּל, וְנוֹדֶה לְּךָ עַל הָאָרֶץ

After grain products:
וְעַל הַמִּחְיָה. בָּרוּךְ אַתָּה ח', עַל הָאָרֶץ וְעַל הַמִּחְיָה.

After wine:
וְעַל פְּרִי הַגֶּפֶן. בָּרוּךְ אַתָּה ח', עַל הָאָרֶץ וְעַל פְּרִי הַגֶּפֶן.

After fruit:
וְעַל הַפֵּרוֹת. בָּרוּךְ אַתָּה ח', עַל הָאָרֶץ וְעַל הַפֵּרוֹת.